Evolutionary Algorithms for Food Science and Technology

Metaheuristics Set

coordinated by
Nicolas Monmarché and Patrick Siarry

Volume 7

Evolutionary Algorithms for Food Science and Technology

Evelyne Lutton
Nathalie Perrot
Alberto Tonda

WILEY

First published 2016 in Great Britain and the United States by ISTE Ltd and John Wiley & Sons, Inc.

ISTE Ltd
27-37 St George's Road
London SW19 4EU
UK

www.iste.co.uk

John Wiley & Sons, Inc.
111 River Street
Hoboken, NJ 07030
USA

www.wiley.com

Library of Congress Control Number: 2016950824

British Library Cataloguing-in-Publication Data
A CIP record for this book is available from the British Library
ISBN 978-1-84821-813-0

Contents

Acknowledgments

We would like to express our gratitude to all those who provided support, read, wrote, offered comments, allowed us to quote their remarks and assisted us in the editing and proofreading of this book. In particular:

– our co-workers, who contributed to some chapters of this book: Sébastien Gaucel, Julie Foucquier, Alain Riaublanc (Chapter 3); André Spritzer (Chapter 4); Olivier Barrière, Cédric Baudrit, Bruno Pinaud, Mariette Sicard, and Pierre-Henri Wuillemin (Chapter 5);

– Nathalie Godefroid for our exciting discussions and her valuable help in writing the preface of this book;

– Corinne Dale for her kind, patient and erudite proofreading;

– our editors Nicolas Monmarché and Patrick Siarry for their friendly insistence that helped us to finish this book.

Preface

This book, which focuses on the domain of food science, is an excellent occasion to consider various issues related to optimization. Optimality, in any domain, is an open question, raising various complex issues. Questioning the purpose of optimization, its ability to answer important real-life questions, is in essence an intellectual exercise: are we able to address the appropriate issues with the help of modern computational tools? Do we believe too much in computation? Are we able to address the right issues with the right tools?

These questions have been considered with the help of a philosopher, Nathalie Godefroid[1], and this preface is the result of our conversations on this vast subject.

The sources

The idea of optimization has its roots in what has been called "modernity" since 16th and 17th Centuries, based on a fundamental change in the perception of man within nature. During Antiquity and the Middle Ages nature was considered a "cosmos", that is a big whole, symbolic, sacred, and respected hierarchy (each creature has its

---

1 Nathalie Godefroid teaches philosophy at undergraduate level (Lycée de Villepreux, France). She also works on aesthetics, and got a first from Paris-CNSM in musical aesthetics (in 1994, class of Rémy Stricker).

own position). "Modernity", however, initiated a neutral standpoint, from which symbolics are progressively removed. The universe is infinite, without purpose, and nature is just a set of physical laws that can be understood and controlled, and therefore submitted to human needs and desires. Descartes' project is to become "owner and master" of nature (*Discours de la méthode*, [DES 37]): managing and predicting natural phenomena becomes an attractive and reachable challenge. This control of nature is based on mathematics: "nature is a book written in mathematical language" (Galilée, [MAR 02]), the aim is to depart from mistery and contingency using rationality and mathematics.

This humanist project (knowledge and progress must benefit human beings, their freedom and their happiness), however, is, the source of other troubles, as highlighted by Heidegger. Technique progressively becomes unlimited, mandatory and above human beings, their projects and activities. Everything then becomes a product, a consumer good, including humans: everything behaves in a way that is "computable". Heidegger shows that technique is no longer an instrument at the service of humans, but an end in itself. The search for performance and optimization is a technical ideal. Rationality in technique is relying on a value system (an evaluation function) in connection with economic interests. The technical means thus dictate a value to the user: efficacy. Efficacy has gained supremacy everywhere: economy, pedagogy, sport, research, social organization, politics, sex, everyday life, etc. "The technical phenomenon is the concern of the immense majority of men today, that is to search in everything for the most efficient method" [ELL 77].

Technique, power and language

With technique, men control nature using a complex and evolving set of means. "Not merely its application, but technique itself is domination – over nature and over men: methodical, clairvoyant domination. The aims and interests of domination are not additional or dictated to technique from above – they enter into the construction of the technical apparatus itself. For example, technique is a social and historical project: into it is projected what a society and its ruling interests decide to make of man and things. The aims of domination are substantive, and belong to the form of technical reason itself" [MAR 64].

Another hazard caused by technique, a major hazard according to Heidegger, is the modification of language: technique triggers the ideal of a non-ambiguous communication language. This ideal language dedicated to information encoding is non-hermeneutic[2], in contrast to natural language, which predates and is external to technique, like the poetic language. This impact of technique on language, with its pure utilitarian approach, is a threat to human essence, as it discards philosophical and religious thoughts, meditations and contemplations, which are typical disinterested, non-measurable activities.

According to the sociologist Philippe Breton (*L'Utopie de la communication*, [BRE 92]), a true social utopia has been built since the Second World War with cybernetics and the work of Norbert Wiener (an American mathematician and philosopher, deemed to be the originator of cybernetics). Considering that everything is information and information sharing, living organisms and machines are on one level: the brain is a computer, thinking is computing... Even if this viewpoint forms the groundwork for artificial intelligence, this posttraumatic utopia emerged after the Second World War, with the intention of discarding such horrors forever. The main values are transparency, consensus and information circulation, as opposed to entropy and chaos. Machines would be more efficient and rational than human beings in making decisions, particularly in politics.

Technical developments thus answer the desire for full control in an uncertain and complex world. But complexities are the essence of life and the human brain's creativity. Randomness and unpredictability are a major characteristic of many systems, including living organisms,

---

2 "Hermeneutics is the theory and methodology of interpretation, especially the interpretation of biblical texts, wisdom literature and philosophical texts. It started out as a theory of text interpretation but has been later broadened to questions of general interpretation." https://en.wikipedia.org/wiki/Hermeneutics.

populations and ecosystems. Creativity of life may remain outside of the scope of mathematical modeling. In Ancient Greek philosophy, an "opportunity" is a recurrent topic: man is the one who knows or should know how to exploit opportunity in a world where nothing is perfectly predictable. Intuition and improvisation are "human" capabilities (in particular in the musical domain, as highlighted by Jankélévitch). Even if computer science and artificial intelligence have made huge progress, the question of the respective roles of man and machine remains.

The human factor in computer science

The human body is synonym of imperfection (Plátõn), flesh is a source of corruption: emotions, illness, death. Medical and technical progress aim at repairing, improving and augmenting the human body. But in the scientific domain, the body is often considered a neutral material, a source of information, of unpredictable data or signals, emptied of its symbolic meaning. Embodiment, the humility of the human condition, and finally the fear of death are at the source of the modern fantasy aiming at abolishing the body. This idea actually also comes from modernity, from Descartes and the first anatomists: humanity is thought; the body, a hindrance. The sociologist David Le Breton ([LE 99]) draws a parallel with the fact that we now use our body less and less in everyday life (cars, lifts, sitting position for working, the Internet, virtual world, etc.): the body has atrophied. This restriction of physical and sensorial activities changes our perception of the world, limits our impact on reality and weakens our actual knowledge of things.

Norbert Wiener was one of the first to blur the line between machine and life. The brain is an intelligent machine that can be mimicked with a computer. The body is inessential, and we may dream of downloading a spirit into a computer, as in some science fiction film ....

But according to Hubert Dreyfus, artificial intelligence underlies some erroneous metaphysics[3] [DRE 79]:

– a biological assumption: "The brain processes information in discrete operations by way of some biological equivalent of on/off switches";

– a psychological assumption: "The mind can be viewed as a device operating on bits of information according to formal rules";

– an epistemological assumption: "All knowledge can be formalized";

– an ontological assumption: "The world consists of independent facts that can be represented by independent symbols".

It has been found that the current understanding of the human mind was based on engineering principles and problem-solving techniques related to management science. Modern artificial intelligence research is now more open to issues that have become important to modern European philosophy and psychology, such as situatedness, embodiment, perception and gestalt.

For the moment, we can still claim that there are fundamental differences between man and machine: the computer has no "marginal consciousness", making man sensitive to various and multiple facts of his environment. The computer is not able to use a context and bring ambiguous words or situations into perspective, making them thus intelligible; it does not distinguish what is essential and what is auxiliary using intuition. The computer is designed for precise works; it is not as versatile and adaptive, as the human brain is. And finally the computer has no body (except maybe if we consider robots).

This question of the role of the body in the implementation of intelligence is a major question. Humans are not facing a world made up of parameters to be recorded and processed. Understanding relies on a symbolic system: language and body. Language is not a code

---

3 Dreyfus' criticism was the source of violent disputes in the AI community in the 1960s–1980s.

made up of unambiguous signs. It is based on culture and history (except maybe for a common core that can be found in all languages, see Noam Chomsky's theories). Words always impart more than their definition; they have an evocative power (now and then magic and religious). The body is a measurement of the world: through his/her body, an individual interprets his/her environment and acts on it according to some influences related to his/her habits or education.

Perception is at the outset of meaning and value-creating, a symbolic comprehension of the world, a deciphering that creates meaning. The viewpoint of a human being is full of feeling, emotions. Intelligence is always in a state that cannot be considered independently from a singular and carnal existence. Human thought is emotional. A computer is a language tool, but not a language subject. It serves a definite purpose.

To conclude, even if the differences between life and machine become increasingly tenuous, such differences still hold because of the corporeal, emotional dimension of life, which is not only an analyzed world, but a perceived one. Abandoning the body would mean forgetting about the flesh and the flavor of the world ... and this point is especially crucial when dealing with food!

Optimization?

Returning to the main topic of this book, optimization is another avatar of modernity: as soon as mathematical models of life and natural phenomena exist or at least seem reachable, the question of control comes about. Control for the benefit of humans, for reducing hazard and uncertainty. Control, or, in other words, optimization.

Optimization comes from the Latin word *optimus* ("best, very good"), and according to a modern dictionary definition[4], optimization is (1) the amount or degree of something that is most favorable to some end and (2) the greatest degree attained or attainable under implied or

———————————

4 http://www.merriam-webster.com.

specified conditions. This actually encompasses a variety of meanings, depending on the scientific or technical domain, on ethics, ideologies and politics... And of course, it may drift and lose its substance: optimization can be used to imprison humans instead of serving them (as expected by the philosophy of the Enlightenment). Famous examples include Taylorism theory, but also contemporary management methods that lead to absurd decision-making, loss of meaning[5], harassment, stress based [COO 98] or lean[6] management.

Promises and limits of computational optimization

So, what do we expect from optimization? Sometimes it is interpreted as an oracle: "it is an optimum", there is no further discussion possible. A mathematical truth. But when dealing with real-world applications, mathematics may not be enough, and the oracle runs up into computational limits. We enter the realm of heuristics, approximate computations. Optimization is no longer foolproof. Answers are given at a computational price that may be huge. Rapid decisions rely on rough approximations and schematic prediction models. The Holy Grail of decision-making transferred to the machine is far from reality: human decision-makers should remain in control in any case. In some applications, the human mind remains more efficient than the computer (for instance in robotic vision or natural language processing). It is clear that humans have some skills that computer programs have not and *vice versa*.

Optimization, and associated computational heuristics like evolutionary computation, are powerful and efficient tools when the context of their use is well designed in accordance with the aims. What do we optimize, what quantity, under what constraints if any, and within what search space? Being conscious of the implicit constraints set on the problem by the very way it is formulated is a crucial step, which is often not well considered enough. Optimization for real

---

5 Christian Morel, http://christian.morel5.perso.sfr.fr/English%20report.pdf.

6 Lean principles come from the Japanese manufacturing industry, and are focused on the elimination of waste.

problems cannot be used as a black box, and finding the appropriate mathematical formalism may be difficult. There may be multiple aims for optimization, and some may be based on subjective assessments (taste, flavor, comfort perception, aesthetics, social acceptance, traditional policies, ethics, etc.). Scale may also be important: what is optimum at a given scale may not be so at another scale, particularly when dealing with "complex systems".

The evaluation utopy

As soon as optimality is considered, we need to how we evaluate the current status of a system, and how we find the equation thereof. Evaluation is highly topical: evaluation is everywhere in our society. According to some expert studies, 95% of large American firms currently use performance control against 45% in 1971; 2015 was even declared "the international year of evaluation"[7].

Once again, philosophers, sociologists and psychologists question evaluation as progress and point out the great dangers of a systematic and quasi-totalitarian evaluation ideology [ABE 11]. Even though evaluation can answer some odd, perhaps narcisstic, need of individuals (to be recognized for the sake of their own personal and social progress), evaluation has been deemed harmful by a number of authors [VID 13], particularly when it is based on economical criteria only. Additionally, for any criterion, whether economic or not, evaluation may tend to uniformization and underestimation of valuable singularities [AND 06]. And, of course, evaluation has a huge technical, computational and social cost: a fair evaluation is extremely complex and time consuming, and in its turn generates a huge amount

---

7 http://www.europeanevaluation.org "International Year of Evaluation 2015: For the first time ever, on December 19 2014, a stand alone UN Resolution on national evaluation capacity development was adopted by the 2nd Committee of the United Nations General Assembly. The Resolution acknowledges 2015 as the International Year of Evaluation and asks each member country to take two landmark steps: (1) strengthen its capacity to conduct evaluations, in accordance with its national policies and priorities and (2) report back to the UN in 2016 on the progress it has made."

of data. This has a cost both in terms of human work (designing, performing, and analyzing evaluations) and in terms of computational needs.

A few theoretical works on evolutionary computation give puzzling answers with respect to this topic. Optimization algorithms based on an approximate computation of the evaluation function have been shown to outperform evolutionary algorithms that compute the complete evaluation, as the latter algorithms lose computational time in the evaluation process [GRE 85]. The rather recent success of "novelty search algorithms" [LEH 11] (evolutionary algorithms not guided by their evaluation function) raises interesting questions about the importance of a systematic and precise evaluation[8].

Quantitative versus qualitative

Evaluation also faces another difficulty: quality assessment may remain qualitative! Translating subjective evaluation into numbers, even with an appropriate scale, is hazardous and highly context-dependent (think of the pain scale in hospitals, where the suffering patient is asked to give a grade on a scale from 1 to 10 to quantify his pain). Qualitative data analysis [LAC 01] is actually an active research topic, particularly in the social science domain.

When it comes to optimization, being able to take into account qualitative data within an algorithm, even very approximatively, is a major advantage, especially in the domain of food science, where subjective quantities are important (taste or flavor, for instance). Few modern optimization approaches allow this. We will see later in this book that interactive evolutionary computation is a convenient framework for this purpose. This rather recent line in research, also called "humanized computation" [TAK 01], actually joins other researches in the domain of visualization and human–computer interactions, aiming at embedding optimization skills within a

---

8 "The main lesson is the inherent limitation of the objective-based paradigm and the unexploited opportunity to guide search through other means."

visualization system. Optimization/visualization is an emerging research topic [JON 13] of particular interest for the food engineering domain.

Once again tricky questions (and difficult associated research questions) arise, regarding the use of subjective evaluation within a computation system. If it becomes possible to take into account a subjective user evaluation within an optimization process, the question of the respective roles of man and machine still holds. The purpose of the optimization itself becomes questionable, as it may lead to undesired outcomes (for instance, a human user drawn into an ocean of information to be evaluated, provided by the machine at an infernal rate). A balance should be found regarding machine and human capabilities, as well as interaction rythms, with the intention of fairly serving human needs.

Issues with complex system

Another point that is particularly salient in food engineering research is the complexity of the systems involved.

What do we mean by complex systems? The complex system research community proposes a definition[9], and optimization plays an important part in this context[10]. The basic idea corresponds to Aristotle's definition: "The whole is more than the sum of its parts". A complex system is a collection of multiple processes, entities, or nested subsystems, where the overall system is difficult to understand and analyze. The emergence of global properties is the result of an imbrication of phenomena occurring at different scales. Nature and living material are rich in fascinating examples of complex systems: ant calories, nervous systems, climate, cell organization or microbial ecosystems.

---

9 Complex Systems Society, http://cssociety.org or http://www.mathinfo.inra.fr/en/ community/complex-systems/presentation.

10 www.courant.nyu.edu/ComplexSystems.

Understanding, controlling and optimizing complex systems is a challenge. The available tools and mathematical models are far from satisfactory. Once again, the limits of "modern" philosophy are obvious. While opening huge topics to research, a complex system approach also forces us to adopt a broader viewpoint, and to take into account uncertainties, randomness and chaotic behavior as intrinsic components.

Optimality in food science

Real-world applications are complex, but they are not the only applications. The questions asked are themselves complex. When dealing with optimization, the evaluation of a complex system state relies on multiple criteria that may be uncertain, messy and subjective. The possible answers deal more with balances and equilibrium states than with the classical notion of the optimum. Often many objectives have to be considered simultaneously.

The vast subject of sustainability, for instance, clearly requires multiobjective optimization tools. The United Nations have adopted the following definition on March 20, 1987: "sustainable development is development that meets the needs of the present without compromising the ability of future generations to meet their own needs[11]". This statement has the major advantage of emphasizing management policies in which economy is not the only concern. But sustainability requires the ability to evaluate a series of criteria, and to propose "optima" that represent compromises between various incompatible aims, like financial profit and the preservation of nature.

Evaluating sustainability in practice is extremely difficult, subjective and scale-dependent. Current techniques such as life-cycle analysis consist of creating an inventory of flows from and to nature for a given system. Such an inventory is supposed to take into consideration every input and output of the system. Then, some impact

11 From A/42/427. Our Common Future: Report of the World Commission on Environment and Development. http://www.un-documents.net/ocf-02.htm.

factors are computed according to international standards (ISO 14000 environmental management standards) and available databases of typical values. Various global environmental impact factors are then computed via weighted sums, and it is generally recognized that a high degree of subjectivity is introduced[12]. These quantities are then used for decision making.

Various criticisms can be made of this type of approach: a life-cycle analysis strongly depends on available data, and databases may become obsolete as new material and manufacturing methods appear. Additionally, even if life-cycle analysis is a powerful tool for analyzing measurable aspects of quantifiable systems, some impacts (human, social, psychological) cannot be reduced to numbers and inserted into existing models. Once again, efficient and versatile computer optimizations are desired for improving the accuracy of existing approaches, but at the same time, it seems clear that in such a context, decision-making cannot be delegated to machines.

Slow optimization

In spite of what can be expected from the acceleration of processors, parallelism and other ultraquick computational frameworks (cloud or GPU computing), a good optimization that efficiently answers highly complex questions remains a slow process based on a back and forth procedure between human design, heavy computations and decision making. A parallel with "slow food" (good, clean and fair food[13]) can be made: as for a consumer of food, it is essential to be

---

12 https://en.wikipedia.org/wiki/Life-cycle_assessment.

13 http://www.slowfood.com.

aware of the processes. Like a consumer assuming a responsive role in the slow food philosophy, a "slow optimization" user should be aware of the context and environment of optimization. The user plays a key role in the optimization process: quality depends on the knowledge put into the design of the optimization task, and into the interpretation of the results. This is particularly obvious in the case of multiobjective optimizations where a Pareto front is provided by the machine, as a set of potential equivalent solutions that the user has to base his final choice upon.

Optimization cannot be used as a fast food. "Our century, which began and developed under the insignia of industrial civilization, first invented the machine and then took it as its life model. We are enslaved by speed and have all succumbed to the same insidious virus: Fast Life. It disrupts our habits, pervades the privacy of our homes and forces us to eat Fast Food." (From the manifesto of international Slow Food movement). More generally, the "slow movement" ideas defend a viewpoint on problem-solving focused on quality instead of on speed and quantity [HON 13], and a right to take time and even fail. "Science needs time to think. Science needs time to read, and time to fail"[14] [JAM 13]. In the same spirit, optimization should be "slow" as well, and consider issues like:

– *Context or "environment"*, or in other terms what contributes to the quality of an optimization: search space, constraints, evaluation criteria and of course human–machine interactions. The algorithms should be versatile enough to respect the needs of the users, and conversely, the user should be aware of the algorithmic limits.

– *Human factor*: algorithms should progress to better embed subjective judgments and needs. The humanized approach [TAK 01] has a significant potential. Optimization algorithm designers should work to provide techniques that are not a "black box" and to allow for fluid user interactions. The availability of a variety of adapted means

---

14 "Since its beginnings, Slow Food has grown into a global movement involving millions of people, in over 150 countries, working to ensure everyone has access to good, clean and fair food." http://slow-science.org.

of interaction is crucial, including visualization, embodiment or even physical visualization [JAN 15].

– *Diversity*: there is rarely a single solution to complex problems. The development of multiobjective algorithms highlights the fact that oversimplification, homogenization and loss of diversity considerably reduce the reliability of results.

– *Responsibility*: delegating decision-making to the machine and trusting algorithmic results too much is not a good strategy. Making decisions is a difficult task. Optimization algorithms provide convenient tools but they give an answer whose quality depends on the quality of the problem settings, the way the question itself is asked, etc.

Because of the increasingly sophisticated and efficient algorithms that are developed, we have the opportunity to improve the quality of our decisions and not only their speeds. Making a good decision takes time, and irresolution is a part of the process.

Evelyne LUTTON
Nathalie GODEFROID
August 2016

1

Introduction

1.1. Evolutionary computation in food science and technology

Food is a major factor for health and public well-being. It is one of the most important sectors of industry and deals with chemicals, agriculture, animal feed, food processing, trade, retail and consumer sectors. Providing an adequate food supply to a growing world population is one of the greatest challenges our global society has to address. Enterprises need to continuously provide safe, tasty, healthy, affordable and sustainable food in sufficient volumes. This requires adapt on to a range of factors, such as the increase in human population and health requirements, and the reduction in crops and livestock due to environmental factors and changes in the sociopolitical scene [VAN 14]. Besides, there is a need for an integrated vision looking at these factors from multiple scales and perspectives:

– from the emotion and pleasure generated when eating food to the nanostructures of a food emulsion or food microbial ecosystems;

– from regional organization to nutritional and sociological impact;

– from health considerations to intercrop culture and microbial complexities, within the human body and in relation to food microbial ecosystems.

Under these conditions, creativity, pragmatism and robust optimization methods are crucial for reaching breakthrough innovations and sustainable solutions. There is a huge opportunity for evolutionary computation, in particular for developing efficient integrative models and decision-support tools [PER 16] to address the aforementioned challenges. Nonetheless, the specific characteristic features of food systems pose a significant challenge to evolutionary computation heuristics:

– the uncertainty and variability (in process, data and available knowledge) that severely influences the dynamics and emergence of various properties;

– the heterogeneity of data, from big volumes at the genomic scale to scarce samples at a more macroscopic level (i.e. process scales). To give an indication of size, an ecosystem of nine microorganisms can be characterized using 40,000 genes, and its dynamics with 10 aromatic compounds;

– the complexity of qualitative and quantitative information, for instance for social and environmental evaluation, at various scales in space and time;

– the variety of perspectives, types of models, research goals and data produced by conceptually disjointed scientific disciplines, ranging from physics and physiology to sociology and ethics.

1.2. A panorama of the current use of evolutionary algorithms in the domain

The potentials of evolutionary optimization methods for the resolution of complex problems in the food domain are demonstrated by a number of publications. A 2004 overview on optimization tools in food industries [TAR 05] mentioned the community interest in evolutionary approaches. Important journals such as the *International Journal of Food Engineering*, *Journal of Food Process Engineering* and *Journal of Food Engineering* regularly publish papers based on evolutionary techniques (more than a dozen papers per year in the last 10 years).

The main focus of these works is issues related to modeling using various model schemes. Evolutionary optimization is mainly used for building models (structure and parameter learning) or exploring the behavior of models, to find some mono- or multiobjective optima, for decision-making purposes (sustainability issues).

There are also other applications, for instance for classification or signal detection [BAR 06], that used genetic algorithms (GAs) to identify the smallest discriminant set of variables to be used in certification process for an Italian cheese (validation of origin labels), or genetic programming to select the most significant wave numbers produced by a Fourier transform infrared spectroscopy measurement device in order to build a rapid detector of bacterial spoilage of beef [ELL 04].

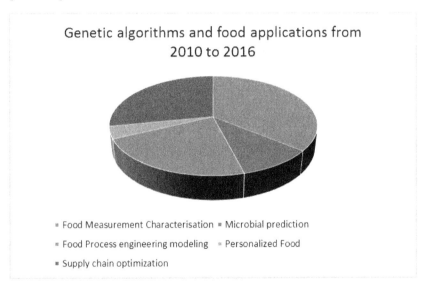

Figure 1.1. *Genetic algorithms and food applications from 2010 to 2016. Research focuses on the core collection of the Web of science, with the topics* (genetic algorithm) *and* (food) *and research domains* (computer science) *or* (engineering) *or* (food science technology); *403 records. For a color version of this figure, see www.iste.co.uk/lutton/algorithms.zip*

An analysis of the current publications related to evolutionary optimization in food science provides an interesting panorama. Evolutionary algorithms (EAs) are rather commonly used for single and multiobjective optimization for various purposes, including constrained optimization and modeling (structure and/or parameter learning). The multiobjective non-sorting genetic algorithm II NSGA-II tool is regularly cited. EA techniques are also often coupled with artificial neural networks, response surface models or fuzzy expert systems. Figure 1.1 highlights five main topics for the period 2010–2016:

– *Decision support for supply chain optimization*: on this topic, evolutionary computation is used as a pure optimization tool to provide optimal solutions for difficult, and often multiobjective, problems related to decision making. [NAK 16] is a typical example: the aim is to manage both the quality of perishable products and product cost (in this paper, GAs have been compared to simulated annealing). Work on the development of biodiesel and other alternatives to petroleum fuels also relies on multiobjective evolutionary optimization. See, to find the case study presented in [WOI 14], where GAs are used to find an optimal economical, environmental and social biodiesel production design from soybean oil.

– *Non-destructive measurement of food*: the focus here is on the use of EAs for learning predictive models by turning the learning task into an optimization. This topic is well represented in the literature. The models can be of any type, from white-box models that strongly rely on a precise knowledge of the underlying mechanisms (differential equations or other explicit mechanistic models) to black-box models. For example, for measuring the loss in apple moisture content during conservation, [TRI 14] use a GA to learn neural networks (NNs). Both the structure and weights of a NN are optimized by a GA with the help of a variable length genotype. Experimental results show the predictive model has high precision. There are many other applications based on similar strategies, for example [ABB 12], applied to predict the properties of wheat-flour dough. Partial least square (PLS) models are also widely used, like in [LIU 14], where it is used to extract relevant information from a near-infrared hyperspectral image; or like in [RAD 15], where it is used for predicting the sugar content of potatoes; or even in [GHA 14] for the qualitative characterization of beer.

– *Food microbial detection and prediction*: as mentioned earlier, EAs are used for learning about various models of microbial food contamination. The models considered are mostly NN and PLS, models, as in [FEN 13], where near-infrared measurements are used. There are also more sophisticated model combinations, like in [ALG 15] where a NN is coupled with a neuro fuzzy inference system to predict the population dynamics of *Pseudomonas aeruginosa* in a complex food system.

– *Food process modeling for process optimization*: in this category, EAs are not only used as discussed previously to build models (model learning), but also to run models, in order to find optimal conditions (model exploration). Here, a model can be used response surface method (RSM) as in [AGH 11], applied to optimize spray dryer operational conditions for the production of fish oil microcapsules. The aim is to simultaneously get the highest values for both encapsulation efficiency and energy efficiency. NNs are also a favorite tool in this category, as, for example, in [MOH 11a] for modeling the oil content of pretreated fried mushrooms, or in [MOH 11b] for modeling and then optimizing a process for dehydrating of carrot slices.

– *Personalized food*: EAs are also used for building decision support systems for personalized diet advice. For example in [LEE 15], a model relying on fuzzy sets and linguistic rules is learned (structure and parameters) using a GA.

Sustainability is a particularly challenging task for evolutionary computation. Multiobjective methods are quasi-mandatory for dealing with incompatible constraints. Datta *et al.* [DAT 07], for instance, propose an evolutionary multiobjective strategy with three objectives for the ecological management of soils: maximization of economic return, maximization of carbon sequestration and minimization of soil erosion. The use of evolutionary computation for eco-design is rather common in domains like architecture[1], or ecology [CHE 10]. In the agrifood domain, however, issues are so complex that the vast majority of work does not rely on optimization heuristics but on manual trial-and-error processes referring to huge international databases of process evaluations. There is a huge field of application for interactive and multiobjective EAs.

---

1 See http://eccogen.crai.archi.fr/wordpress/publications/.

1.3. The purpose of this book

This book is an attempt to address some questions related to optimization in the specific domain of food science. We try to show how evolutionary computation tools pave the way to new solutions because of their versatility and robustness, and by offering new ways to better integrate what can be called the "human factor".

After a brief introduction to EAs, three examples from our own experience are presented in order to illustrate some new usages of EAs in food science, with a focus on the issues related to human expertise and to co-operative co-evolution strategies.

A first example is given in Chapter 3, where it is shown that a visualization of the behavior of an EA during optimization yields important information for modeling. This simple experiment stresses the fact that an appropriate visualization is important for understanding and revisiting model design and data-fitting steps. Within an iterative modeling process, expert users play an important role, and efficient and appropriate visualizations are important for the ease of the process.

User interactions can be more closely integrated into a computational process than a succession of autonomous computations followed by user interaction. Chapter 4 presents a modeling tool based on an interactive EA.

Finally, Chapter 5 develops two strategies for dealing with modeling issues based on cooperative–co-evolution schemes, another way of performing optimization with an EA.

2

A Brief Introduction to Evolutionary Algorithms

"Ce n'est qu'en essayant continuellement que l'on finit par réussir.
Autrement dit: plus ça rate, plus on a de chances que ça marche."
Devise Shadok

"Only by continually trying we finally succeed.
In other words: the more it fails, the more likely it will work."
Shadok motto[1]

The above motto is a good summary for evolutionary algorithms (EAs) and for stochastic searches in general: a repetition of random trials till the optimum is reached. Of course, there is a bit more to it than that, a hint of "intelligent" control in these algorithms.

More seriously, EAs, also known as genetic algorithms (GAs), evolution strategies (ESs), evolutionary programming (EP) or artificial evolution, are stochastic optimization methods based on a simplified model of natural evolution, according to Darwin's theory. This chapter

---

1 The Shadocks are antropomorphic characters of French animated films created in 1968. They are sort of birds, which are rather aggressive and stupid, and act according to a series of mottos, demonstrating a great surrealist absurdity, see https://fr.wikipedia.org/wiki/Les _Shadoks.

proposes an overview of these methods, with a focus on their extreme versatility, which is one of the reasons for their success in a large variety of application domains. It has to be noted that artificial evolution is not limited to pure optimization applications, as there are other uses of these techniques, in particular when they are embedded in an interactive framework. Implementations of EAs are, however, computationally expensive, and a fine apperception of artificial evolution mechanisms helps to efficiently tune their various components. The most efficient applications of EAs are often based on hybridizations with other optimization techniques. What is learnt by experience is that EAs should not be considered a competitor in opposition to other stochastic or deterministic optimization approaches, but rather as a complementary framework that makes it possible to orchestrate the cooperation of various approaches in parallel.

2.1. Artificial evolution: Darwin's theory in a computer

The observation of biological phenomena is a rich and fruitful source of inspiration for computer science. GAs are an excellent example of this cross-fertilization. Grouped for about 20 years under the umbrella-term "evolutionary algorithm", a full family of GA-like algorithms have been proposed whose fundamental principles are a simplification of Charles Darwin's theory. The idea is to imitate within a program the capability of a population of living organisms to adapt to its environment using selection and genetic inheritance mechanisms. A great number of problem-solving methods and stochastic optimization methods have been developed according to these principles, which correspond to what is now called "artificial Darwinism". The term actually covers a whole set of techniques: GAs, ESs, EP and genetic programming (GP). Each of these methods differs slightly according to the way Darwinian principles are translated into the artificial model. The common ingredients of these approaches are a population (that represents, for instance, points in a search space) and a set of stochastic operators (see Figure 2.1). The simulated evolution is generally organized into generations, and mimics genetics in a very simplified way. The engines of this evolution are:

– *selection*, that relies on evaluation of the "quality" of an individual with respect to what is searched for, usually embedded in a single function, called the *fitness function* and;

– *genetic operators*, usually called crossover and mutation, that generate new individuals for a new generation.

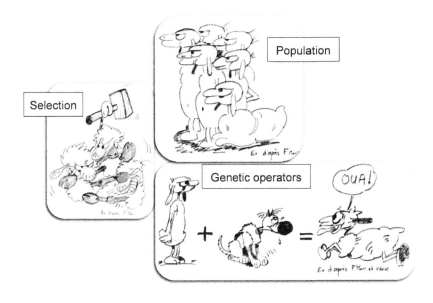

Figure 2.1. *Ingredients of an EA: a population, a selection mechanism and a set of stochastic operators*

The efficiency of an EA is measured in terms of population convergence into what is expected, which is most often the optimum quality measurement function. A large part of theoretical research on EAs is focused on this problem of convergence in order to better understand what makes the task easy or difficult for an EA (the notion of EA-hard or EA-easy problems). We will see in the sequel that some encouraging theoretical answers exist: an EA converges toward the optimum fitness function if some simple rules are respected. Other crucial issues remain open, like the convergence speed, for instance. We can, however, comfortably claim that the efficiency of EAs as a stochastic search heuristic has been globally proved from a theoretical standpoint, strengthening practical know-how for about 50 years.

Another important point is that EAs are zero-order stochastic optimization methods: that is, no continuity or derivability properties of the function to be optimized are expected for the method to be run. Only the values of the function on some sample points are used, which makes EAs particularly well adapted to very irregular, complex or difficult functions. The counterpart is the computational cost, which supports the usual recommendation that EAs only be used when other, more classical and deterministic optimization heuristics are deceived and trapped in local optima. This holds, for instance, for very large search spaces, functions that are too irregular, and mixed variables (symbolic, numeric). EAs are also useful in other cases when the function varies with time (dynamical problems) or when human expertise needs to be considered (interactive problems).

Despite the apparent simplicity of an evolutionary process, building an efficient EA is not easy. EAs are very sensitive to parameter and algorithmic settings, and particularly to the way in which the problem is conditioned: this latter issue is sometimes called "representation". Efficient design needs a good knowledge of the problem to be solved, a clear understanding of the EA mechanisms and creativity: it is an error to consider an EA as a magic black box that provides an answer as soon as enough computational resources are provided. Having said that, evolutionary approaches are not far from being part of our everyday lives. Their scope of application is actually very large, and various success stories are based on evolutionary optimization[2].

2.2. The source of inspiration: evolutionism and Darwin's theory

The notion of natural evolution is a very old idea, and in Greek Antiquity several authors proposed interpretations of the world in

---

[2] See, for instance, the Eureqa software http://nutonian.wikidot.com, or the HUMIES contests in the GECCO conference series: http://sigevo.saclay.inria.fr.

terms of "evolutionism": the struggle for life, randomness and adaptation to the environment[3].

During the Renaissance period and the 17th Century, various intermediary hypotheses emerged between the religious dogma of species created once and for all by God, and a diversification of species under environmental influence. The first attempt to express the principles of evolution the was made by the geometrist philosopher Maupertuis, around 1750, who talked about hereditary variations and selection. Lamarck, follower of Buffon, was the first who proposed a theory for evolution, according to two principles: the need creates the organism, and characteristics acquired under environmental influence are transmitted from generation to generation.

The publication of *The Origin of Species* by Charles Darwin in November 1859 questioned the notion of species. Until then species were considered immutable ("fixism"), at most likely to form strains, an essential feature that justifies the necessity to design a catalog as proposed by Linnaeus. Darwin's famous expedition on the *Beagle* from 1831 to 1836 traveling to South America, the Pacific, Australia and New Zealand was the occasion for him to systematically observe many lineages of species. The native species of the Galapagos Islands drew his attention to the extreme variability of species, emphasized by geographic isolation, and the fierce competition for life:

> "It may be said that natural selection is daily and hourly scrutinising, throughout the world, every variation, even the slightest; rejecting that which is bad, preserving and adding up all that is good; silently and insensibly working, whenever and wherever opportunity offers, at the improvement of each organic being in relation to its organic and inorganic conditions of life." [DAR 59].

---

3 *"Ainsi dès l'antiquité, se manifestent plusieurs conceptions d'importance: hiérarchie des êtres vivants et gradation naturelle (Aristote); production de l'harmonie organique par le hasard et la mort (Empédocle, Démocrite, etc ...); lutte des vivants pour la vie (Lucrèce)."* [ROS 32].

According to Darwin, natural evolution is governed by the three following principles [GRI 99]:

– the principle of variation: among individuals within any population, there is variation in morphology, physiology and behavior;

– the principle of heredity: offspring resemble their parents more than they resemble unrelated individuals;

– the principle of selection: in a given environment, some forms are more successful at surviving and reproducing than others.

Evolution is based on random modifications that are inherited by organisms. Beneficial changes are kept while others disappear by natural selection: a weak organism has less chances than a better adapted one to get food, reproduce and thus transmit its genes.

Many biologists and philosophers followed and opposed Darwin's theory and proposed variations around the basic notions of Darwinism. Mutationism, for instance, proposed by Hugo de Vries (1848–1935) considers discontinuous variations inspired from Mendelian laws, and embedded in the gene pool [VRI 10].

Mutationism and other evolutions of the Darwinian model have converged since 1930 onto what is now called the synthetic theory of evolution[4]. Evolutionism also developed in sociology and ethnology with the sometimes controversial aim of building models of social development and complex societies.

2.3. Darwin in a computer

The translation of Darwinian evolutionary principles into global optimization heuristics was made independently on both sides of the Atlantic Ocean in the 1960s, based on the central idea of a population-based adaptation or collective learning ability. The two trends evolved in parallel with their own fields of application,

---

4 https://en.wikipedia.org/wiki/Portal:Evolutionary_biology.

conferences and journals. By the end of the 20th Century, the generic term EAs was accepted as a consensus.

The growing appeal of these methods to researchers and industrials is correlated to the increase in computation power, the availability of parallel computation solutions (grid, cloud, GPU processors), and the diffusion of programming toolboxes (MatLab, SciLab, R, C, Java or specification languages like EASEA[5]).

The "American" school, initiated by John Holland in the 1960s, is the historical source of GAs [HOL 75]. Built for dealing with discrete optimization problems, they have been extended to continuous domain optimizations [JON 75]. In Germany, almost simultaneously, methods called ESs were proposed by Rechenberg [REC 73], then by his follower Schwefel [SCH 75] (see [HOF 91]). These methods were designed for dealing with continuous optimization problems and have been symmetrically applied to the discrete domain [REC 89].

The main criticism of evolutionary approaches is their lack of theoretical background, in particular regarding their global convergence. Building a theory about these population-based stochastic processes is actually a very challenging task, and convincing convergence theorems arose rather late (see section 2.5).

GAs are still the best known EA approaches, because of the books by David Goldberg [GOL 89]. However, the publication of the book of John Holland in 1975 [HOL 75] marks the date these techniques entered the public domain. This book gathers together a series of ideas he had been developing since the 1960s [HOL 62]. Some of his students from Michigan University followed: Bagley [BAG 67], Caviccio [CAV 70] and Rosenberg [ROS 67]. A history of the domain can be found in [FOG 98, GOL 89] and [DAV 91a].

---

5 http://easea.unistra.fr.

2.4. The genetic engine

The components of the "canonical" EA presented in this section are very simple, but they should be considered a basic "recipe". Efficient implementations of EAs are more complex, as we need to adapt, or even create, operators that correspond to the specifics of the problem, in the same way that a recipe taken from a (possibly French!) cooking book needs fine adaptation to guests' taste, available materials and ingredients to be truly enjoyed.

2.4.1. Evolutionary loop

An EA is organized according to a generational loop (see Figure 2.2) that governs the way a population of individuals is transformed into the next one. When dealing with optimization, an individual usually represents a possible solution to the problem, that is a point of the search space [DAV 87, GOL 89, MIC 92]. The main steps in this loop are the following:

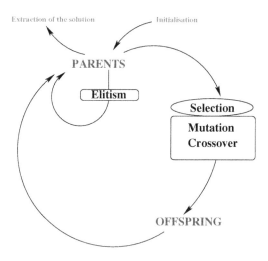

Figure 2.2. The EA loop

– *Initialization*: initial populations are usually randomly chosen in the absence of prior information. Solutions coming from expertise or obtained using a deterministic greedy fast algorithm, for instance, can be embedded in the initial population to facilitate convergence. Even if in theory an EA converges from any initial state toward the global optimum, in practice, a fair sampling of the search space is extremely important to ensure a good exploration capability and a fast convergence. This is particularly crucial when dealing with complex and high dimensional search spaces.

– *Evaluation*: this step computes the quality of the individuals with respect to the problem to be solved. This quality measurement is usually embedded in a single function called the *fitness function*. This function is optimized (maximized or minimized) along the evolution of the algorithm. No hypothesis is set on the fitness function (no derivability nor continuity condition), the only request is that a probability of selection can be built from it.

– *Selection*: the task of this operator is to detect which individual of the current population will reproduce (be a "parent") and in which proportion. Selection is based on a probability distribution built from the fitness function. In the canonical GA "*à la* Goldberg" [GOL 89], two parents are selected and produce two children, thus a number of parents equal to the desired number of offspring is selected. Of course, other schemes are possible. The main parameter of this step is the *selection pressure*, which is the quotient of the probability of being selected for the best individual over the probability of being selected for an average individual. This parameter is important for balancing the exploration–exploitation tradeoff of the algorithm: a high selection pressure may provoke a premature convergence, while a low selection pressure may let the search stagnate.

– *Reproduction*: parent individuals generate offspring via two main mechanisms called genetic operators. *Crossover* combines two parents while *mutation* modifies one individual. These operators are applied randomly according to probabilities p_c and p_m which are fixed or vary along evolution. These probabilities are important for tuning the EA. They have a big influence on the quality and speed of convergence (once again for balancing the exploration–exploitation tradeoff).

– *Replacement*: this step aims at building the population for the next generation. Experimental and theoretical analyses have shown that a naive approach of a full replacement of parents by offspring is less efficient than a strategy that maintains a "memory" of the past best candidate solutions. Common replacement strategies consist of keeping a proportion of the best individuals of the population unchanged. This is sometimes called *generation gap* [JON 75] or *replacement percentage*. This parameter is another important setting for tuning an EA. In this respect, ESs propose an elegant framework for dealing with this issue: with a population of size μ that generates λ offspring, two strategies can be adopted:

1) a (λ, μ) strategy, where the replacement percentage is fixed and tuned by the value of $\mu - \lambda$;

2) a $(\lambda + \mu)$ strategy, where the replacement percentage varies according to the quality of the offspring: an intermediate pool of size $\lambda + \mu$ is created, from which the μ best ones are kept for the next generation.

Note that the "+" scheme can also be used for $\lambda > \mu$: for instance, a $(1 + 10)$ scheme creates 10 offspring from one individual, compares then to the current best solution and keeps the best of all for the next generation.

It is also possible to get rid of the notion of generation (for parallel implementation in particular) and program a *steady-state EA* that maintains a population of fixed size but each time a new individual is created, an individual from the current population is discarded according to a *reverse selection* process, to statistically replace the worst individuals in the population with new ones:

– *End of the loop*: a stopping criterion is not always available, particularly when the target value of the optimum is not known. An appropriate tuning of this criterion is often delicate. When no information is available, a common strategy is to stop the algorithm after a given number of iterations (computing resource limit reached), or when an obvious stagnation state is detected. Stagnation is reached when the diversity of the population goes under a threshold, or when no improvement in the best solution has been observed for a given number of generations.

The previous process is highly tunable and the main parameters are population size, crossover and mutation probabilities, selective pressure, generation gap and stopping criterion. A careful tuning of the genetic engine may allow us to go from a very inefficient and computation time-wasting architecture to a very efficient algorithm. Tuning takes time and should not be neglected if an efficient EA is expected.

2.4.2. *Genetic operators*

The genetic operators directly depend on the choice of a representation: this feature can be used to categorize the different strands of EAs (GAs, ESs, GP, grammatical evolution (GE), etc.). The few classical representations used in the domain are presented below, but the literature proposes many other representations for non-standard search spaces such as graphs, lists or images, for instance.

2.4.3. *GAs and binary representation*

Even if these methods use real encoding now, discrete and binary encoding are the historical characteristic of GAs. Each individual, or candidate solution to the optimization problem, is represented as a fixed-length binary chain, whose elements (called *genes* or *alleles*) belong to a finite set of values. This representation is well suited to deal with some combinatorial problems, but can also be used on continuous search spaces, with a regular sampling. In this case, the length n of the string is an important parameter that tunes the precision of the sampling and, as a consequence, the precision of the result (up to $1/2^n$) [VÉH 93].

Implementations on binary strings, that is on $\{0, 1\}^n$, are still used in a systematic way, as Holland [HOL 75] argued that a binary alphabet (the smallest possible one) is optimal, according to his schema theory. This has been questioned by many authors since. Goldberg [GOL 89], for instance, introduced the notion of *code complexity*, explaining that from a practical viewpoint the choice of coding is a tradeoff between alphabet size and code complexity. Grossly speaking, this notion of complexity deals with the relation between a modification in the code space (a mutation) and its result in the search space. In other words, to imitate nature, we speak about *genotype* (the code) and *phenotype* (the point of the search space). This interesting notion raises the attention to issues linked with representation: is a mutation actually a small modification? How are the neighborhoods of a point in the codes space and in the search space correlated? Another important constraint is the algorithmic complexity of a coding/decoding step: these steps are executed a huge number of times when the algorithm is running. An inefficient and expensive encoding may drastically reduce the GA efficiency.

Binary crossovers (Figure 2.3) mix the parents' genomes in mimicking natural chromosome breeding processes. Similarly, mutation (Figure 2.4) introduces some errors into the genetic code. Intuitively, a crossover tends to concentrate the population around "good" individuals, while mutation tends to push individuals, into unknown areas. Mutation and crossover probabilities are a way to balance the exploration and exploitation capabilities of a GA, but this balance the is usually made empirically.

Regarding exploration ability, it has been experimentally and theoretically proven [DAV 91] that mutation limits *genetic drift*, that is a loss in diversity due to selection in small populations. The mutation is usually low and fixed along generations. Some decreasing mutation probability schemes, inspired by theoretical proofs of convergence [DAV 91] are used to accelerate convergence, imposing more exploration at the beginning of the search and more exploitation at the end.

2.4.4. *ESs and continuous representation*

Continuous or real representations are historically linked to numerical optimization researches [SCH 95]. The search space is R^n or a part of it, and genetic operators may have geometric interpretations. Blend crossovers, BLX-type [ESH 93], generate a random barycentric offspring x' from two parents, x and y, in R^n

because of a random value α chosen between 0 and 1 or between $-\epsilon$ and $1 + \epsilon$ as follows:

$$x' = \alpha x + (1 - \alpha)y \qquad [2.1]$$

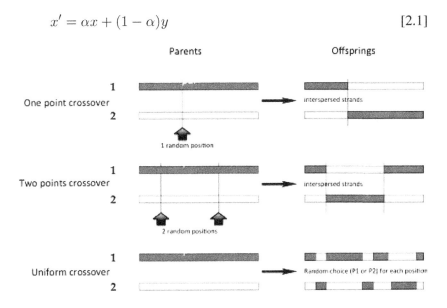

Figure 2.3. *Some simple binary crossovers. Crossover probability p_c is defined for a couple of individuals*

Figure 2.4. *Simple binary mutation: the GA mutation probability p_m is often defined with respect to genes and not to individuals. A random number generation with probability p_m is performed for each position on the genome to decide if this position is going to be flipped in the offspring*

This operation can be performed component-wise (i.e. with an α independently chosen for each component) to get a better mixing of x and y. This type of crossover can be generalized to more than two parents, or even to the whole population ("global crossover" [SCH 95]).

Various mutation schemes save been proposed and tested. The ones listed below are the most frequently used in practice:

– *Gaussian mutation* adds a Gaussian noise to the components of the vector-individual x. An additional parameter thus needs to be tuned: σ, the standard deviation. As above, σ can be defined component-wise (anisotropic mutation) or globally (isotropic mutation):

$$x' = x + N(0, \sigma) \hspace{3cm} [2.2]$$

– *adaptive mutation* aims to automatically tune the above additional parameter σ, making it dependent on generation number or fitness value;

– *log-normal self-adaptive mutation* delegates the job to evolution by integrating σ into the genetic material of the individual, which becomes (x, σ). The search is performed in R^{n+1} for an isotropic scheme or in R^{2n} for an anisotropic one:

$$\sigma' = \sigma exp(N(0, \tau)) \text{ and } x' = x + N(0, \sigma) \hspace{2cm} [2.3]$$

The parameter τ has been experimentally proven to be less sensitive [SCH 95];

– *uniform mutation* is a coarser approach inspired by the GA scheme that replaces a random component of the vector-individual by a random value in its validity interval. This operator is efficient in cases where it is important to maintain a good diversity (rough landscapes). It is often used in synergy with other, more "concentrating", operators.

There are many other specialized mutation operators dealing with constrained optimization. A comprehensive review can be found in [BAN 97].

2.4.5. *GP and tree-based representation*

GP corresponds to variable length representations structured as trees. It has been designed originally to manipulate Lisp programs [KOZ 92] with the intention of creating programs without human intervention ("automatic programming"). The richness of the tree representation is one of the reasons for the success of these methods.

Many problems (optimization, command, control) can be formulated as program induction problems.

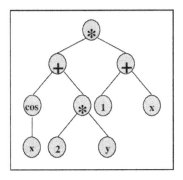

Figure 2.5. *A GP tree that represents the function*
$$((\cos(x) + 2 * y) * (1 + x))$$

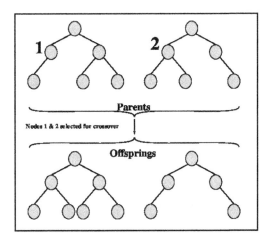

Figure 2.6. *A GP crossover*

A GP explores the search space of programs recursively built from a set of functions and a set of terminals (variables, constants, data). The individuals are programs that are executed in order to be evaluated. Crossovers are simple subtree exchanges (see Figure 2.6) and mutations are more specific, according to the effect they have on trees (Figure 2.7):

– supression or the addition of a node;

– modification of the function of a node, with respect to its arity;

– Gaussian mutation of the constants (continuous values);

– mutation of the discrete variables, by permutation or uniform mutation.

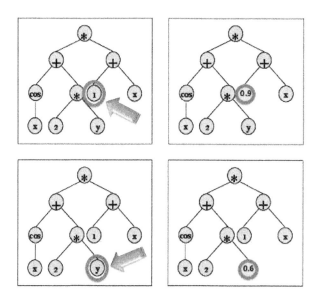

Figure 2.7. *GP mutations. Top: an intratype mutation. Bottom: an intertype mutation*

A known problem occurring in GP is the "bloat" – a saturation of the memory space due to rapid growth of the tree's size during evolution (bias toward complex solutions, overfitting). Various strategies have been developed to deal with this effect. The most simple strategies consist of limiting the trees size [SOU 96, LAN 00b].

GP is used in many application domains [KOZ 92]: for symbolic regression (evolving a mathematical expression in order to fit a set of sample points), for optimal control, for action and trajectory planning in robotics, for learning differential equations [GAU 14], and of course in food process modeling (see Chapter 5).

2.4.6. *GE and grammar-based representation*

In nature, gene expression – or more precisely the expression of proteins encoded in genes – seems to be rather independent from the gene position in the chromosome. This independence with respect to the gene's position may be a desirable feature in some combinatorial problems. GE has been built to mimic this natural feature. GE uses a variable length representation, that, because of a translation stage based on a grammar (Backus Naur form), produces complex individuals that respect some validity criteria. All classical genetic operators can be applied as genes have a simple structure. A detailed description of GE can be found in [ONE 03].

2.4.7. *Selective pressure*

The selection step is the only place where the fitness function is considered. The bridge between optimization and simulated evolution is this fitness function. The fitness function represents the adaptation of the individual to its environment: in this, evolution progressively promotes individuals that bear a "good" fitness. If fitness represents a function to be optimized, the job is done. The way fitness is used in the selection process does not necessitate any strong hypothesis on the function, like continuity or derivability. As said before, we just need to build a procedure that transforms fitness into a probability of selection going in the right direction (the higher probabilities for the best fitness).

A simple implementation is the *proportional selection* that results in a probability $P(i)$ that the individual i from a function f will be maximized as follows:

$$P(i) = f(i) / \sum_{k=0}^{SizePop} f(k) \qquad [2.4]$$

where $SizePop$ is the size of the population.

The selective pressure, usually measured as the relative selection probability of the best individual with respect to an average individual, has a huge importance on the diversity of the population. Too much pressure causes a depletion of diversity in the population, which is often the reason for a premature convergence of the algorithm. Not enough pressure reduces efficiency, and tends to let the algorithm behave like a pure random search. Proportional selection is sensitive to the relative values of f, and the resulting selective pressure varies along computation, depending on the content of the current population.

There are selection strategies that control the selection pressure to better balance exploration and exploitation capabilities of the EA:

– *fitness scaling* explicitly rescales f at each generation so that the resulting probability corresponds to a desired scale, that is $Max(P(i)) = C(1/SizePop) \sum_{k=0}^{SizePop} P(k)$, with C usually fixed between 1.2 and 2;

– *ranking* affects the selection probability according to the rank each individual of the population has with respect to f;

– *tournament* keeps the best individual from a small random subsample of the population. The selective pressure depends on the size of the subsample T. $T = 2$ to 5 are typical values.

2.5. Theoretical issues

EAs are quite complex to build, are usually computationally expensive, and, as said above, their use as a black box is not recommended. Their efficiency depends on a subtle balance between exploration and exploitation capabilities, random and controlled components. These techniques behave like a semiblind sampling process: randomness makes it robust while focus makes it efficient; too much randomness is a waste of time, while too much focus makes it prematurely converge.

Theoretical works on EAs attempt to answer several important questions regarding these stochastic search algorithms: why and how do they converge, at which speed, and what is easy or difficult?

Since the 1960s several theories have emerged, and we notice an increase in interest in the last 20 years from mathematicians, particularly in the stochastic models and dynamical systems that are appropriate to deal with this very complex topic.

The first theory of global convergence was proposed by John Holland [HOL 75, GOL 89]. The *schema theory* is actually a very simple model, valid on infinite sized population and during the first steps of the algorithm. This approach has been largely disputed as relying on rather unrealistic hypotheses from a practical viewpoint (in particular regarding the action of the crossover and mutation operators), but the schema theory proposes a simple and intuitive interpretation that is the origin of many clever algorithmic improvements and a series of "rules of thumb" for parameter tuning. Some of Holland's intuitions have been confirmed by rigorous theoretical and experimental works.

Local convergence results have been proposed in parallel for ESs, in particular in Schwefel in Dortmun's team [BAE 91, BEY 00]. Global convergence results based on dynamical systems [ALT 95, ALT 00, CER 95], Markov modeling [DAV 91, HOR 93, NIX 92, VOS 90] or according to statistical physics models [PRU 01, SHA 96] were also proposed. These provide more precise results on the dynamics of finite-size populations, but the models are still simplified.

More precise results can also be obtained if additional hypotheses are set on the fitness functions. Controlled fitness landscapes have been largely considered in the EA community: NK-landscapes and tunable fitness landscapes [REE 00], $(1, \lambda)$-ES on a simple function [BEY 01], for instance. In these cases, the behavior of some simple EA engines is easier to analyze. Additionally, genetic engine characteristics set a specific topology on the definition domain: for the same fitness function, two different EA engines (for example with or without crossover) may have very different behavior. According to the induced topology, the corresponding fitness landscape may look drastically different. The terms "fitness landscape" thus involves both the profile of the fitness function on its definition domain and the search paths produced by the genetic operators. As a result, useful quantities for modeling EAs should be measured with respect to this "genetic" topology. For regularity measurements, the same holds: irregularity characteristics must be measured with respect to an underlying measure based on the genetic operators' effect [LEB 98, LAN 00a]. In other terms, the neighborhood system that serves as a basis for the calculation of regularity exponents, for instance, should be linked with transition probabilities via the genetic operators. It is thus more precise to talk about fitness landscape irregularity, instead of fitness function irregularity [LUT 06a, LUT 06b].

2.6. Beyond optimization

It is actually possible to do more than pure optimization with EAs, i.e. keeping the best individual from the last generation as an approximation of the optimal solution. We give some examples in the following that use artificial Darwinism mechanisms in different ways, where notably diversity management has a preponderant role.

2.6.1. *Multimodal landscapes*

When the fitness function has several global optima, a classical EA converges randomly onto one of the optima. However, in some applications it is useful to get information about the position of all equivalent (or almost equivalent) optima. Simple extensions of the EA model, based on the imitation of the natural phenomenon of *niching*, use an implicit or explicit management of subpopulations (also called niches here).

A first set of methods simply consists of *reinforcing diversity* in the populations [GOL 87]. The idea is to favor the emergence of distinct species using a modification of the replacement step to avoid aggregation of individuals in areas that have already been explored. An additional notion is used: similarity of genomes for deciding which parent replaces which offspring ("crowding scheme" [GOL 89, JON 75] or unicity operators based on a Hamming distance [MAU 84]).

The most common method however is the *sharing scheme* [GOL 87, GOL 89] that uses an interindividual distance at the selection level. If individuals of the same subpopulation have to share the same resources, the growth of this population is limited; and when overcrowding occurs, individuals tend to search other areas to in which to settle. The sharing scheme is based on a notion of neighborhood. The fitness function is reduced proportional to the number of neighbors of an individual, $\sharp\mathcal{N}(i)$:

$$f'(i) = \frac{f(i)}{\sharp\mathcal{N}(i)} \text{ with } \mathcal{N}(i) = \{k \in Pop, d(i,k) \leq T\} \qquad [2.5]$$

There are also methods that explicitly define subpopulations [COH 87], sometimes hosted on separate processors or *islands*, that exchange individuals at fixed time intervals. This island-based scheme is now largely used in parallel implementations of EAs [LUT 14a].

2.6.2. *Co-evolution*

It is sometimes possible to formulate a problem as a collective learning task, the searched solution then being built from the whole evolved population and not only from the best individual from the final population. Co-evolutionary algorithms (CEAs) have been developed in different ways and are generally defined as a class of EAs in which the fitness of an individual depends on its relationship to other members of the population. The most fundamental classification relies on the distinction between cooperation and competition. In cooperative algorithms, individuals are rewarded when they work well with other individuals, and are punished otherwise. In competitive algorithms, individuals are rewarded at the expense of those with which they interact. Most work on CEAs has been in competitive models; there has however, been a increased interest in cooperation to tackle difficult optimization problems by means of problem decomposition [KAU 92, HUS 91, BOU 01, COL 00].

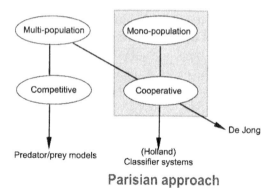

Figure 2.8. *Taxonomy of co-evolution strategies*

The proposed approaches can actually be divided into approaches that have a single population of interbreeding individuals, and those that maintain multiple interacting populations (see Figure 2.8) [OCH 07]:

– *Single-population approaches*: the earliest single-population method that extended the basic evolutionary model to allow the emergence of co-adapted subcomponents was the classifier system [HOL 77], a rule-based learning paradigm that evolves fixed-length stimulus-response rules. A generalization of this paradigm for solving complex problems was proposed in [COL 00], where an aggregation of multiple individuals (in a single population) is considered for solving the inverse problem for iterated function systems. In this approach, which has been called Parisian evolution, an additional fitness measure (a "local" fitness) is used to independently evaluate the subcomponents during the search process, while a "global" fitness is used at each generation to gauge the progress of the aggregate solution. This scheme is well suited for incorporating additional or incomplete information about the solution searched. However, in order to avoid trivial and degenerate solutions, a special mechanism for maintaining population diversity should be devised. Successful applications of the Parisian approach can be found in the image analysis and signal processing literature [BOU 01, DUN 06], in data retrieval applications [LAN 06] and for food process modeling, as described later in Chapter 5.

– *Multiple-population approaches*: the first people to apply a multispecies cooperative co-evolutionary approach to tackle a difficult optimization problem were Husbands and Mill [HUS 91], who successfully co-evolved job-shop schedules, using a parallel distributed algorithm. A few years later, the work by Potter and De Jong [POT 00] helped popularize the idea of cooperative co-evolution as an optimization tool. The authors devised a multiple-population framework where a decomposition of the problem into subcomponents could be identified. Each component is assigned to a subpopulation that evolves simultaneously but in isolation to the other subpopulations. The fitness of an individual in a given subpopulation is calculated after selecting team mates from the other subpopulation in order to form a complete solution. Note that diversity in the ecosystem in this framework is naturally achieved through maintaining genetically-isolated populations. This framework has been further analyzed [PAU 02] by considering a relationship between cooperative co-evolution and evolutionary game theory, and thus studying it from a dynamical system perspective. From the problem-solving point of view, multispecies cooperative co-evolution has been applied, for instance, to neural network and concept learning [DEJ 07, POT 00], and to inventory-control optimization [ERI 97].

2.6.3. *Multiobjective optimization*

In some applications, the quantities to be optimized are difficult to embed in a single fitness function, particularly when several, sometimes incompatible criteria are involved, for instance maximizing the strength of a mechanical part while minimizing the weight and its production cost. When no information about the relative importance of the various criteria and constraints is available, multiobjective optimization is a solution. The notion of Pareto dominance is then central: in the case of maximization of a set of n criteria f_i, solution x_1 dominates solution x_2 if and only if:

$$\forall k \quad f_k(x_1) \geq f_k(x_2) \quad \text{and} \quad \exists j \quad f_j(x_1) > f_j(x_2) \qquad [2.6]$$

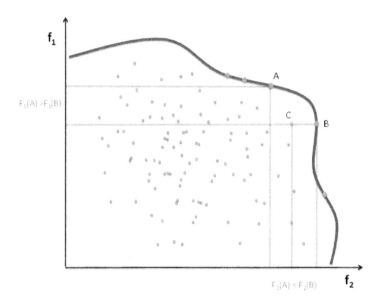

Figure 2.9. *Pareto front in the case of a maximization in two dimensions. Point C is dominated by A and B, but A does not dominate B, and* vice versa: *A and B belong to the Pareto Front. For a color version of this figure, see* www.iste.co.uk/lutton/algorithms.zip

A solution to a multiobjective problem is then a set of solutions, called the *Pareto front*, corresponding to all non-dominated solutions in the search space. A Pareto front is the set of all acceptable trade-offs between the n criteria f_i, thus a set of potential answers to the problem. In such cases, decision making is delegated to another often user-driven level.

Multiobjective EAs converge toward the Pareto front because of a small modification of the classical scheme. The selection procedure is adapted in order to favor non-dominated solution, while maintaining a good level of diversity inside the population in order to efficiently sample the Pareto front and avoid degenerated solutions where the population concentrates on a single point. A comparative study of multiobjective EAs is proposed in [ZIT 00] and a commonly used method is NSGA-II [DEB 00].

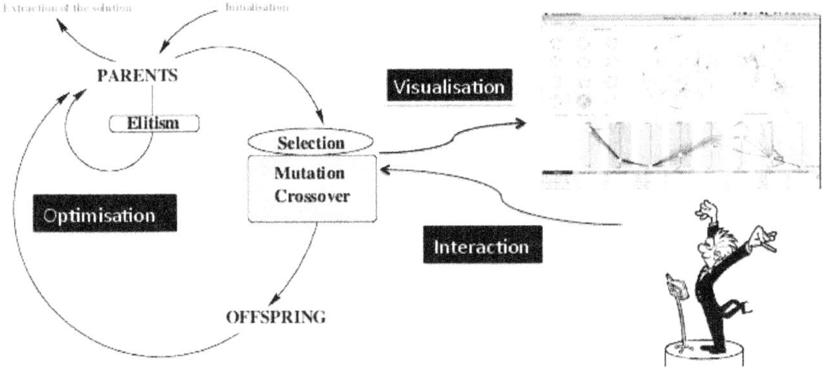

Figure 2.10. *Interactive evolution. interaction can occur at various levels. Usually the interaction entry point is via a human–computer interface, and via data visualization. For a color version of this figure, see www.iste.co.uk/lutton/algorithms.zip*

2.6.4. *Interactive optimization*

When what is expected to be optimized is not precisely defined, classical optimization strategies are not efficient. As we have seen for multiobjective optimization, where the optimization problem becomes ambiguous due to the fact that the various criteria cannot be prioritized and merged in a simple way, EA techniques can provide interesting solutions. The problem becomes even more difficult when a non-measurable quantity has to be considered in the optimization process. It then becomes useful to integrate a human user in the evolutionary loop. This configuration was first considered about 20 years ago as "interactive evolution" or "humanized computation".

The idea of a *humanized computational intelligence* consists of directly embedding the capability of a human in a computational system, instead of using a representative model as a more classical artificial intelligence approach. In other terms, this approach aims at dealing with complex problems by combining human capabilities with autonomous computations, leveraging the strengths of both sides [TAK 98].

The use of interactive evolution algorithms (IEA or interactive evolutionary computation) is the most common approach for humanized computation. This strategy considers the user as the provider of a fitness function (or part of it) inside an evolutionary loop (see Figure 2.10). Early work in interactive evolution [ANG 96, SIM 91b, SIM 91a, TOD 92] was oriented toward art and design. IEAs are now used in many applications [BAN 97]. Characteristic applications include, the adaptation of auditive aids [TAK 99] or cochlear implants [LEG 07], control law design of human-like movements in robotics [KAM 97], Web page design [MON 99] and data retrieval [TAK 08, SIM 08].

There are, however, different ways to interlace human interaction and optimization computations that may be as simple as an iterative scheme or as sophisticated as collaborative learning and problem-solving using serious games or crowd sourcing [BEL 09, VOU 11, POT 10]. An interesting feature of these latter approaches is that they consider various tools to deal with what they call "user engagement", which may represent a new source of inspiration to address the well-known "user fatigue" issue of IEAs.

3

Model Analysis and Visualization

Obtaining reliable *in silico* food models is fundamental for a better understanding of these systems. The complex phenomena involved in these real-world processes are reflected in the intricate structure of models, so that thoroughly exploring their behavior and, for example, finding meaningful correlations between variables has become a relevant challenge for the experts. In this chapter, we present a methodology based on visualization and evolutionary computation to assist experts during model exploration. The proposed approach is tested on an established model of milk gel structures, and we show how experts are eventually able to find a correlation between two parameters, previously considered independent. Reverse engineering the final outcome, the emergence of such a pattern is proved by the physical laws underlying the oil–water interface colonization. It is interesting to note that, while the present work is focused on milk gel modeling, the proposed methodology can be straightforwardly generalized to other complex physical phenomena. The work described in this chapter has been done with Sébastien Gaucel, Julie Foucquier and Alain Riaublanc and published in [LUT 14b].

3.1. Introduction

Building *in silico* models for food processes is an important but difficult task, as there are various known bottlenecks [PER 11]. The process of model design, for instance, often relies on computationally-expensive optimizations to match a theoretical model with available data (parameter learning). Scarcity of data is a classical source of trouble for the optimization process, resulting in badly conditioned problems. Solutions provided by optimization cannot be exploited directly and must be revisited by experts in order to disambiguate equivalent sets of solutions. Facilitating high-level expert analysis of computational results, or the interaction of expert knowledge with computational processes, is a challenging task. Interactive optimization is an active field of research [TAK 98], and its potential applications in the domain of food process modeling are numerous.

Name	Description	Unit
m_p	Total mass of proteins in the solution (constant)	g
m_{wp}	Mass of native whey proteins in the solution	g
m_{cas}	Mass of casein micelles in the solution	g
S_0	Initial lipid surface	m^2
$S_{f_{all}}$	Lipid surface available for adsorption of both native whey proteins and casein micelles	m^2
$S_{f_{res}}$	Lipid surface left by casein micelles due to steric effects for native whey proteins	m^2
k_{wp}	Adsorption rate of native whey proteins	s^{-1}
k_{cas}	Adsorption rate of casein micelles	s^{-1}
s_{wp}	Surface area occupied by 1 g of native whey proteins	$m^2.g^{-1}$
s_{cas}	Surface area occupied by 1 g of casein micelles	$m^2.g^{-1}$
α	Fraction of the adsorbed surface of a casein micelle reserved for native whey proteins	dimensionless
$w_{wp}(0)$	Initial mass percentage of native whey proteins in the solution, $w_{wp}(0) = m_{wp}(0)/m_p(0)$	%
$w_{cas}(0)$	Initial mass percentage of casein micelles in the solution, $w_{cas}(0) = m_{cas}(0)/m_p(0)$	%
$w_{wp_{int}}$	Final mass percentage of native whey proteins at lipid interface relative to the total mass of adsorbed proteins	%
$w_{cas_{int}}$	Final mass percentage of casein micelles at lipid interface relative to the total mass of adsorbed proteins	%
Γ	Final interfacial concentration which corresponds to the quantity of adsorbed proteins per 1 m^2 of lipid surface	$mg.m^{-2}$
$d_{3.2}$	Average diameter of lipid droplet	m
ρ_l	Lipid density	$g.m^{-3}$
m_l	Mass of lipid (constant)	g
μ	Population size parameter for the evolutionary algorithms used in the experience	dimensionless
λ	Offspring size parameter for the evolutionary algorithms used in the experience	dimensionless
$\eta_{operator}$	Distribution index for a genetic operator in the NSGA-II evolutionary algorithm	dimensionless

Table 3.1. *Glossary that will be used in this chapter*

Optimization tools are often used in a "black box" manner, and computationaly optimal results may then yield an imprecise, ambiguous or even incorrect parameter setting. In this chapter, we present a methodology based on evolutionary algorithms (EAs, also known as "genetic algorithms", GAs). Their iterative, population-based, algorithmic structure, if appropriately exploited, allows various features of the search space, which correspond to possible pathologies of the highlighted model considered. Experts may have access to these pathological features via appropriate theoretical analysis, as soon as they know what to search for. As we will see below, the observation of the successive population distributions of the EAs gives us some ideas about the possible degeneracies of the model searched, thus making the task of the expert easier. We exemplify this approach on a complex test case with the prediction of the structure of a milk gel.

As discussed in Chapter 2, considering evolutionary optimization as a "black box" is not a good strategy in general. A first reason is that we may lose the opportunity to adapt the mechanisms to the specifics of the problem, which usually improves the efficiency of the algorithms and reduces its computation time. Another reason is related to the internal mechanisms of the algorithm that perform a sampling of the search space via the evolution of its population. Observing how the population is distributed, then concentrated along generations; how diversity is lost or how it persists; the appearance of the optimal set of solutions (a point or a significant subset): all these factors provide important information about the nature of the optimization problem. In the case of model learning, this analysis makes it possible, for instance, to know if the learning set is large and discriminative enough.

Classical uses of EAs only consider the best individual from the last population as an estimation of the optimum, and do not exploit all useful information provided by the algorithm, that may help assess whether the optimum is correct and robust. A recent work points out the potential benefit of visualizing data collected during the execution of an EA [LUT 11a, LUT 11b], and shows how a multidimensional visualization tool, GraphDice [BEZ 10], can help to efficiently navigate inside the dataset collected during the execution of an EA. In this chapter, we follow the research line previously described, and develop the proposed methodology for the specific case of a milk gel model.

Oil-in-water emulsions are dispersed systems stabilized by surface-active molecules, including proteins, polymers, ionic and non-ionic surfactants [DIC 11]. Proteins, as the main emulsifier in food systems, adsorb to the freshly formed interface of oil droplets created during homogenization. They stabilize the emulsion because of their ability to generate repulsive interactions (steric and electrostatic) between oil droplets [MCC 04]. Milk proteins have excellent emulsifying properties and are one of the most convenient ingredients used in food processing [SUR 14, DIC 99]. Recent research on milk gels [DIC 01, MUR 02, GAY 09, KNU 08, DIC 11] highlights the major role of nanoscopic and microscopic dynamics during interface stabilization on the qualitative characteristics of the gel, both macroscopic and nutritional. Although the structural characteristics of pure protein aggregates submitted to heat treatment are widely studied [RAB 11], research on aggregates of casein coupled to whey proteins (whether denatured or not) is still in the initial stages [MOR 12]: the interpretation of surface composition in emulsions containing the full range of aggregated milk proteins (caseins and whey proteins) is quite complex and certainly not yet fully resolved. And if experimental data about the phenomena are collected, they are still rarely exploited in modeling approaches.

Among the main research lines on milk gel, an important part is devoted to the development of models with the ability to replicate the dynamics of gel formation at relevant scales, linking the structure to macroscopic properties. Thus, these models aim at including all levels and correctly predicting the complex interactions between elements at different scales [ERN 11]. For instance, the colonization of the lipid droplet interface at the nanoscopic and microscopic scales (from the size of surfactants like whey proteins, with a diameter around 3 nm, to micelles and aggregates, with a diameter around 100 nm) influences the formation of milk polymers: to predict the properties of the product at a macroscopic level, such as consistency, some direct knowledge on this process is needed. Although modeling approaches have started to address this multiscale reconstruction problem [FOU 12], there is considerable space for improvements. To cope with the scarcity of data, we propose an approach combining computational exploration, based on an EA, with visualizations of the results.

3.1.1. *Experimental data*

Data have been collected during two emulsification experiences, where the continuous phase of the emulsion is formed by disolving milk proteins in permeate. The milk proteins considered are the following:

– a mixture of caseins (Promilk 852B, IDI, France, with 5% moisture, 1.5% fat, 85.5% nitrogenous matter/dry matter, 8.5% mineral matter, 4% lactose, 81% nitrogenous matter in powder, 92% casein micelle, 2.6% Ca, 1.5% P, 0.3% K, 0.1% Na and 0.1% Mg);

– native whey proteins (BiPro, DAVISCO, Minnesota USA, with 5% max. moisture, 95% min. protein, dry basis, 1% max. fat, 3% max. ash, and 1% max. lactose, pH between 6.7 and 7.5) with milk permeate powder (Armor Proteines, France, with a pH of 6.0 min., 3% max. moisture, 3% min. proteins, 1% max. fat, 82% lactose, and 8% ashes).

The continuous phase has been prepared the day before the test, stirred at 4 °C and then heated at 60 °C before emulsification. The dispersed phase of the emulsion is a saturated liquid: anhydrous milk fat that has been heated at 60 °C to become liquid.

Two sets of experiments were carried out to characterize the emulsification dynamics (so-called database 1 and database 2). They differed in the homogenization process and in the volume of emulsion produced. The process for database 1 consisted of mixing of 49 g of the protein phase and 21 g of milk fat using a rotor stator homogenizer and a low-pressure homogenizer (50 bar). The process for database 2 consisted of mixing of 182 g of the protein phase and 78 g of milk fat using a blender and a high-pressure homogenizer (300 bar). Although they produced different amounts of emulsion, 70 g and 260 g for databases 1 and 2, respectively, the proportions of the different components were kept constant: 30% w/w of milk fat and 70% w/w of water phase leading to about 3.4% w/w of proteins. Several initial conditions were tested, and the emulsions characterized using measurements at the micro-/nanoscale [FOU 11, SUR 14]:

– laser light scattering was used to measure the diameter of the lipid droplets in the emulsion and evaluate the size distribution. For database 1, measurements were performed using a Saturn DigiSizer 5200 (Micromeritics, Norcross, USA), while for database 2, they were made with a LS 13320 Laser Diffraction Particle Size Analyser (Beckman Coulter California, USA). The gathered information was used to compute the initial free lipid surface S_0. The measurement error for the aforementioned devices was around 10%;

– for database 1, the composition of the interface of lipid droplets was studied using the Patton and Huston technique [PAT 86] to separate droplets. The interfacial protein concentration was then quantified through the Markwell method [MAR 78]. Subsequently, SDS-PAGE electrophoresis was applied to determine the concentration of each protein at the interface. In database 2, SDS-PAGE electrophoresis was carried out and gels were purchased from Invitrogen Ltd (Paisley, UK). The measurements gave the interfacial concentration (Γ) and the percentage of adsorbed caseins ($p_{cas_{ads}}$). The measurement error of the Patton techniques and the electrophoresis were each around 10%. The resulting measurement error for this experimentation was thus around 20%.

Database 1 was used for learning and database 2 for validation, see Table 3.2: the training set was made up of seven samples, L_1 to L_7, and four samples were used as the validation set, V_1 to V_4.

Sample	$w_{cas}(0)$ (%)	$d3.2$ (μm)	$m_p(0)$ (g)	$w_{cas_{int}}$ (%)	Γ ($mg \cdot m^{-2}$)	Database
L_1	13	0.6	2.47	5	5.6	1
L_2	19	0.7	2.44	9	4.8	1
L_3	21	0.6	2.42	16	4.0	1
L_4	26	0.65	2.40	43	4.9	1
L_5	32	0.55	2.40	65	5.6	1
L_6	49	0.56	2.39	71	4.2	1
L_7	80	0.9	2.37	84	9.3	1
V_1	13	0.59	8.79	0	4.66	2
V_2	22	0.74	8.47	33	4.4	2
V_3	31	0.87	8.64	46	6.88	2
V_4	80	0.75	9.18	91	6.93	2

Table 3.2. *Milk gel data used for training (Database 1, L_1 to L_7) and validation (Database 2, V_1 to V_4)*

3.1.2. *Modeling milk gel competition at the interface*

Figure 3.1 gives an overview of the model used to test our approach. The model, developed in a previous work [FOU 11], was chosen because of the availability of data and expert knowledge on the process behavior. It is important to note that the focus of this chapter is on the coupling of evolutionary computation and visualization techniques, not on the model itself, or its efficiency: the proposed approach can be generalized to any kind of model.

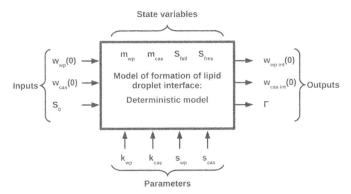

Figure 3.1. *Model of milk gel formation. For a color version of this figure, see www.iste.co.uk/lutton/algorithms.zip*

The amount of native whey proteins in the solution, m_{wp}, and casein micelles, m_{cas}, as well as the surfaces S_{fall} and S_{fres} evolve with time. S_{fall} is the lipid surface area available for colonization of native whey proteins and casein micelles, and S_{fres} is the lipid surface left by casein micelles, owing to steric effects, for native whey proteins.

The model predicts the structure characterized by the mass percentage of adsorbed casein micelles and native whey proteins relative to the total amount of proteins adsorbed at the lipid interface, $w_{cas_{int}}$ and $w_{wp_{int}} = 1 - w_{cas_{int}}$ respectively, and the interfacial concentration, Γ, which corresponds to the quantity of adsorbed proteins for 1 m^2 of lipid surface. These outputs depend on:

– the structure of the model built from expert knowledge;

– the parameters of the model, i.e. five parameters: adsorption rate of native whey proteins, k_{wp}, adsorption rate of casein micelles, k_{cas}, surface occupied by 1 g of native whey proteins, s_{wp}, surface occupied by 1 g of casein micelles, s_{cas} and fraction of the adsorbed surface of a casein micelle left for native whey proteins, α. k_{wp} and k_{cas} are associated with a mean representation of the reactions that take place at a local level according to the organization of each protein at the nanoscale. It induces specific diffusion and protein–surface interactions that are taken into account at a higher scale through these overall parameters. s_{wp} and s_{cas} are associated with a mean representation of actual adsorption, conformational reorganization and structural consolidation that take place at a lower scale level;

– the inputs, i.e. the initial mass percentage of casein micelles in the water phase, w_{cas_0}, initial mass percentage of native whey proteins in the water phase, $w_{wp_0} = 1 - w_{cas_0}$, initial mass of proteins $m_p(0)$, initial mass of lipid $m_l(0)$, and initial lipid surface S_0 depending on $d_{3.2}$ (average diameter of lipid droplets):

$$S_0 = \frac{m_l}{\rho_l} \frac{6}{d_{3.2}} \qquad [3.1]$$

where m_l is the constant mass of lipid in the solution and ρ_l is the lipid density (0.920×10^6 g $\cdot$ m^{-3}).

The system described in equations 3.2 is an ordinary differential equation system that can be solved with a Runge–Kutta fourth-order method [BUT 87].

$$\begin{cases} \frac{dm_{wp}}{dt} = -k_{wp}m_{wp}\left(\frac{m_{wp}}{m_{wp}+m_{cas}}\right)\frac{S_{f_{all}}+S_{fres}}{S_0} \\[2mm] \frac{dm_{cas}}{dt} = -k_{cas}m_{cas}\left(\frac{m_{cas}}{m_{wp}+m_{cas}}\right)\frac{S_{f_{all}}}{S_0}\left(1-\frac{(m_{cas_0}-m_{cas})s_{cas}}{S_0}\right) \\[2mm] \frac{dS_{f_{all}}}{dt} = \frac{dm_{wp}}{dt}s_{wp}\left(\frac{S_{f_{all}}}{S_{f_{all}}+S_{fres}}\right)+\frac{dm_{cas}}{dt}s_{cas} \\[2mm] \frac{dS_{fres}}{dt} = \frac{dm_{wp}}{dt}s_{wp}\left(\frac{S_{fres}}{S_{f_{all}}+S_{fres}}\right)-\frac{dm_{cas}}{dt}\alpha s_{cas} \end{cases} \qquad [3.2]$$

Initialization of the state variables is set by using Table 3.2 and the following relations with S_0 computed according to equation [3.1]:

$$m_{wp}(0) = m_p(0)\, w_{wp}(0)$$

$$m_{cas}(0) = m_p(0)\, w_{cas}(0)$$

$$S_{fres}(0) = 0$$

$$S_{f_{all}}(0) = S_0$$

3.1.3. *Learning the parameters of the model using an evolutionary approach*

The learning task can be turned into the following optimization problem: find the optimal parameter setting that best matches the training dataset. To run an EA on such a problem, the following features have been fixed:

– *Search space, structure of an individual of the population*: a candidate solution is a vector of real numbers, describing the values of model parameters k_{wp}, k_{cas}, s_{wp}, s_{cas} and α. An individual is thus a set of five real values in the $(0, 1)$ interval: each value is mapped in the appropriate interval of validity for the corresponding parameter, before evaluation. A complete list of intervals is given in Table 3.3.

– Fitness function, how to assess the quality of a solution: the quality of a solution is given by the average squared error between values predicted by the system of equations [3.2] (solved using a Runge–Kutta fourth-order method) and experimental data (learning set). It is important to note that the model has several outputs, and a candidate solution might perform very well for one output, and badly for the others. In this experiment, we are focusing on two outputs. The interfacial concentration and the final casein percentage in the mixture. There are two ways to consider this: single-objective and bi-objective approaches, as EAs are also able to deal with multiobjective problems [DEB 01].

Parameter	Minimum	Maximum
k_{wp}	0	100
k_{cas}	0	100
s_{wp}	0	1,500
s_{cas}	0	300
α	0	1

Table 3.3. *Intervals of validity for each parameter in the optimization problem considered. The parameters' values are obtained from literature and expertise on the subject*

– Genetic engine, operators and reproduction strategies: given the problem characteristics, we chose two established EAs particularly suited to study the nature of the problem: covariance matrix adaptation evolution strategy (CMA-ES) [HAN 03] and non-sorting genetic algorithm II (NSGA-II) [DEB 02]. CMA-ES is considered one of the best real-value optimizers for single-objective problems, delivering high-quality results in a very limited amount of time. NSGA-II is the *de facto* state of the art for multiobjective optimization.

Both algorithms are purposefully set with a large population in order to obtain more insights on the nature of the problem from the distribution of candidate solutions in the search space. For CMA-ES, the fitness function to be minimized is the product of the average squared errors on each output; NSGA-II simply considers the average squared error on each output as an objective to minimize. Complete parameters for both algorithms are reported in Table 3.4.

CMA-ES		NSGA-II	
Parameter	Value	Parameter	Value
Objective	$minimize(f0 * f1)$	Objective 1	$Minimize(f0)$
		Objective 2	$Minimize(f1)$
Stop condition	Stagnation (10^{-12})	Stop condition	100 generations
μ	250	μ	500
λ	500	λ	500
Initial points	0.5	P(crossover)	0.9
Initial standard deviations	0.3	P(mutation)	$\frac{1}{problem\_dimension}$
		$\eta_{crossover}$	20
		$\eta_{mutation}$	20

Table 3.4. *Parameters of the two EAs used during the experience. μ is the size of the population, and λ is the size of the offspring generated at each iteration. While NSGA-II is terminated after 100 iterations (or generations), CMA-ES stops when a stagnation condition is reached (when the difference in fitness value between all solutions in the population is under a user-defined threshold). For CMA-ES, initial points in the middle of the search space are specified for each dimension, and initial standard deviation to generate solutions is set; the algorithm will self-adapt the standard deviation during the run. For NSGA-II, P(operator) represents the probability of applying a specific genetic operator when a new solution is produced. $\eta_{operator}$ is the distribution index of the genetic operator, regulating how much the child solutions will differ from the parents*

For every algorithm, a single run is performed, until a stagnation condition is reached (for CMA-ES) or 100 iterations of the process have expired (NSGA-II).

3.1.4. *Visualization using the GraphDice environment*

GraphDice [BEZ 10] is an evolution of ScatterDice [ELM 08], a multidimensional visual exploration tool that enables the user to navigate in a multidimensional set via simple two-dimensional projections, organized as scatterplot matrices. The visual coherence between various projections is based on animated three-dimensional transitions. A scatterplot matrix presents an overview of the possible configurations, thumbnails of the scatterplots, and support for interactive navigation in the multidimensional space. Various queries can be built using bounding volumes in the dataset, sculpting the query from different viewpoints to become more and more refined. Furthermore, the dimensions in the navigation space can be reordered, manually or automatically, to highlight salient correlations and differences[1].

GraphDice [BEZ 10] uses the same principles but with many additional features allows the same type of data (.csv files), and other more sophisticated formats to be read as it also embeds graph visualization utilities[2]. GraphDice can be used to visualize data collected during the run of an EA [LUT 11a]. At each generation, the content of the current population can be written into a .csv file as shown in Figure 3.2, creating what can be called a "cloud" of successive populations made up of multidimensional points. The figures presented in the following section have been generated using EvoGraphDice, another extension of GraphDice specially devised to analyze dependencies between variables (an extension of a principal component analysis of multidimensional data, based on an interactive EA, allowing us to consider various linear or nonlinear dependencies) [CAN 12].

The visualization system (Figures 3.3–3.9) displays:

– an overview scatterplot matrix (top left, entitled "Overview") showing the original dataset of seven dimensions, namely generation, fitness and five parameters, plus additional dimensions (1.7) for EvoGraphDice;

– a main plot view (top right), corresponding to a zoom in on one of the cells of the overview scatterplot matrix. It corresponds to the red cell at the intersection of the green line and columns in the scatterplot matrix;

– a tool bar for the main plot view giving access to zoom, convex hulls and other functionalities;

---

1 A demo of ScatterDice can be launched from http://www.aviz.fr/~fekete/scatterdice/. It accepts standard .csv files (although it may be necessary to add a second line after the header giving the data type for each column – INT, STR, REAL, etc).

2 A demo of GraphDice is accessible at http://www.aviz.fr/graphdice/.

– a selection query window to manage various subsets of points that are interactively selected (lasso selection using the mouse).

```
Generation;Fitness;Chromosome0;Chromosome1;Chromosome2;Chromosome3;
    Chromosome4
INT;DOUBLE;DOUBLE;DOUBLE;DOUBLE;DOUBLE;DOUBLE
0;29.0424;0.552813;0.57205;0.329723;0.810545;0.134889
0;10000;0.608819;0.717563;0.638848;0.111938;0.761085
0;4.23809;0.355794;0.754131;0.176697;0.314317;0.925262
0;10000;0.472549;0.392627;0.763183;0.338806;0.286481
0;10000;0.454194;0.815799;0.805686;0.311948;0.791315


...
```

Figure 3.2. *A simple .csv file collected during a run of the single-objective EA (CMA-ES). Chromosome0; Chromosome1; Chromosome2; Chromosome3; and Chromosome4 are k_{wp}, k_{cas}, s_{wp}, s_{cas} and α respectively*

3.2. Results and discussion

3.2.1. *Sensitivity analysis*

A global sensitivity analysis was performed in [FOU 11] on the basis of the variance-based method described in [SAL 02]. The results are summarized in Table 3.5. The relation $w_{cas_{int}} + w_{int} = 1$ induced identical sensitivity results for output variables $w_{cas_{int}}$ and $w_{wp_{int}}$. For the sake of clarity, Table 3.5 only presents the results for $w_{cas_{int}}$ and Γ.

This analysis recommends keeping the five parameters relative to the established structure. Regardless of the initial conditions, k_{wp} and k_{cas} seem to have an impact on the variation of the percentage of adsorbed caseins (Table 3.5). Their impact on the variation of the interfacial concentration, however, is verified only for high initial casein percentages. Nevertheless, it is important to find good values for all parameters: k_{wp} and k_{cas} have an impact for at least one given initial condition and one output; α and s_{cas} seem to have a major impact on the variation of the outputs of the model for high initial percentage of caseins; and, for all initial conditions, s_{wp} has a high impact on the variance of the outputs of the model.

S_{T_i}	$w_{cas}(0) = 13\%$		$w_{cas}(0) = 21\%$		$w_{cas}(0) = 49\%$		$w_{cas}(0) = 80\%$	
	$w_{cas_{int}}$	Γ	$w_{cas_{int}}$	Γ	$w_{cas_{int}}$	Γ	$w_{cas_{int}}$	Γ
k_{wp}	++	0	++	0	+	0	+++	+
k_{cas}	++	0	+++	0	++	0	+++	+
α	0	0	0	0	0	0	++++	+
s_{wp}	+	++++	+	+++	+	++	+++	+
s_{cas}	0	0	0	0	+	0	++++	+++

Table 3.5. *Total effects of the parameters on the variations in the outputs of the model. Meaning of symbols: 0, no or very low impact $(S_{T_i} \leq 0.1)$; +, low impact $(0.1 < S_{T_i} \leq 0.3)$; ++, average impact $(0.3 < S_{T_i} \leq 0.6)$; +++, high impact $(0.6 < S_{T_i} \leq 1)$; ++++, very high impact $(S_{T_i} > 1.0)$*

Sensitivity analysis makes it possible to gain some insight into the model, and it is a starting point for the visual exploration. It is evident that five parameters have to be kept for a complete description of the dynamics of the system. However, questions remain about the possible simplifications at equilibrium state.

3.2.2. *Visual exploration of the model*

A mono-objective EA was first run on the five parameters' search space according to the settings presented in section 3.1.3. It is important to note that the available datasets only represent equilibrium states (when $m_{wp} + m_{cas}$ goes to zero): observation results are thus only valid for these specific conditions. A best fitting corresponds to the following values:

$$k_{wp} = 11.976\text{s}^{-1},$$
$$k_{cas} = 80.783\text{s}^{-1},$$
$$s_{wp} = 261.209\text{m}^2 \cdot \text{g}^{-1},$$
$$s_{cas} = 104.876\text{m}^2 \cdot \text{g}^{-1} \text{ and}$$
$$\alpha = 9.748 \times 10^{-12}$$

However, a visual exploration of the EA data collected during the run (a sample file is given in Figure 3.2) shows a convergence toward a rather large area of values for k_{wp}, k_{cas} parameters. The right part of Figure 3.3 displays a projection onto the plane (k_{wp}, k_{cas}) of the distribution of the points visited by the EA along generations. The best fitness values are colored in red. It is evident that, even if the EA is converging in a satisfying manner, there is a whole set of optimal values distributed along a line segment. This evidence is even more salient when examining the same type of data collected during the run of a multiobjective EA (NSGA-II). The main plot (right) of Figure 3.4 shows a zoom on the Pareto front, i.e. the projection defined by the two fitness values (fitness0, fitness1), corresponding to the two aims being optimized (i.e. the average error for adsorbed casein and the average error for interfacial concentration). A set of queries highlight some parts of the Pareto front: preference of fitness0 over fitness1 in green (and *vice versa* in red), and equivalent compromise in yellow. The same color encoding is used in Figure 3.5, which displays projection in the (k_{wp}, k_{cas}) plane of the same dataset. The green area corresponds to a large set of equivalent points (a cone). Yellow points are distributed along the bottom line of the green cone.

Figures 3.3–3.5 show a possible dependence between k_{wp} and k_{cas} for optimal values. Experiments run with only four parameters are presented in Figures 3.8 and 3.9. The four parameters are k, s_{wp}, s_{cas} and α with $k_{wp} = k \cdot k_{cas}$.

Figure 3.8 shows a convergence toward a point with respect to all projections in the four-parameter space, and optimal values are:

$$k_{wp} = 1\,\mathrm{s}^{-1},$$
$$k_{cas} = 6.748\,\mathrm{s}^{-1},$$
$$s_{wp} = 261.264\,\mathrm{m}^2 \cdot g^{-1},$$
$$s_{cas} = 104.786\,\mathrm{m}^2 \cdot g^{-1} \text{ and}$$
$$\alpha = 1.352 \times 10^{-12}$$

It is notable how the values found for s_{wp}, s_{cas} and α are extremely close to values previously found for the five-parameter model. The $\frac{k_{wp}}{k_{cas}}$ ratio is 0.148 for both the five-parameter and four-parameter models. Small differences are due to the stochastic nature of the optimization techniques applied to the problem.

Figures 3.6 and 3.7 show the model fitting experimental points of data, for the five-parameter and the four-parameter models, with optimized parameter values. It is intuitive to note how the shapes of the curves and the points are almost exactly the same. Theoretical analysis of section 3.2.3 confirms this visual evidence.

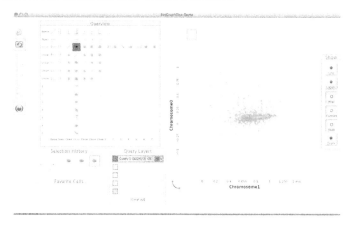

Figure 3.3. *Main window of EvoGraphDice (yellow column and lines numbered 1–7 are additional dimensions computed by the system for the purpose of analysis) for the visualization of data collected during a CMA-ES run searching the five-parameter space. Red points correspond to best fitness values: they are distributed along a line. For a color version of this figure, see www.iste.co.uk/lutton/algorithms.zip*

The observation of average fitting errors per sample for both solutions (Table 3.6 and Figures 3.6 and 3.7) also shows that the prediction of adsorbed casein seems to be an easier task than the prediction of the interfacial concentration.

3.2.3. *Theoretical discussion*

A change in variables has been performed in order to circumvent the mathematical singularity of system 3.2, when $m_{wp} + m_{cas}$ goes to zero. Introducing the $P = \dfrac{m_{wp}}{m_{cas}}$ ratio allows us to rewrite equations [3.2] as an equivalent regular system:

$$
\begin{cases}
\frac{dP}{dt} = \frac{P}{S_0(P+1)} \left[k_{wp} P (S_{fall} + S_{fres}) - k_{cas} S_{fall} \right.\\
\qquad \left. \times \left(1 - \frac{(m_{cas_0} - m_{cas}) s_{cas}}{S_0} \right) \right]\\[2mm]
\frac{dm_{cas}}{dt} = -k_{cas} \frac{S_{fall} m_{cas}}{S_0(P+1)}\\
\qquad \times \left(1 - \frac{(m_{cas_0} - m_{cas}) s_{cas}}{S_0} \right)\\[2mm]
\frac{dS_{fall}}{dt} = -\frac{S_{fall} m_{cas}}{S_0(P+1)} \left[k_{wp} s_{wp} P^2 + k_{cas} s_{cas} \right.\\
\qquad \left. \times \left(1 - \frac{(m_{cas_0} - m_{cas}) s_{cas}}{S_0} \right) \right]\\[2mm]
\frac{dS_{fres}}{dt} = -\frac{m_{cas}}{S_0(P+1)} \left[k_{wp} s_{wp} S_{fres} P^2 - k_{cas} \alpha s_{cas} S_{fall} \right.\\
\qquad \left. \times \left(1 - \frac{(m_{cas_0} - m_{cas}) s_{cas}}{S_0} \right) \right]
\end{cases}
\qquad [3.3]
$$

Model	Average error for adsorbed casein samples		Average error for interfacial concentration samples	
	Training set			
	Absolute	Relative (%)	Absolute	Relative (%)
Four parameters	0.113	14.3	0.773	20.9
Five parameters	0.113	14.3	0.773	20.89
	Validation set			
	Absolute	Relative (%)	Absolute	Relative (%)
Four parameters	0.055	0.06	1.008	44.42
Five parameters	0.055	0.06	1.008	44.38

Table 3.6. *Average errors for four- and five-parameter solutions for both training and validation sets. The relative error for each data point is computed as $\frac{abs(p_i - e_i)}{e_{max} - e_{min}}$, where p_i is the value predicted by the model, e_i is the experimental value, and e_{max} and e_{min} are the maximum and minimum experimental values, respectively*

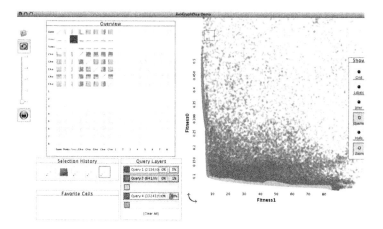

Figure 3.4. *Visualization of a multiobjective run (NSGA-II) in the five-parameter space. Pareto front (right): preference of fitness0 over fitness1 in green (and vice versa in red), and equivalent compromise in yellow. Blue points are non-Pareto optimal. For a color version of this figure, see www.iste.co.uk/lutton/algorithms.zip*

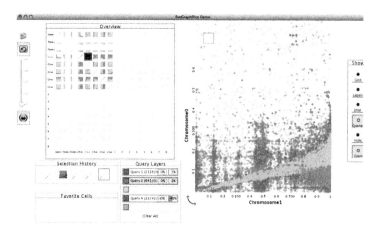

Figure 3.5. *Visualization of a multiobjective run (NSGA-II) in the five-parameter space. (k_{wp}, k_{cas}) projection (right), with the same coloring of the Pareto frontier. Yellow points are at the bottom line of the green cone. For a color version of this figure, see www.iste.co.uk/lutton/algorithms.zip*

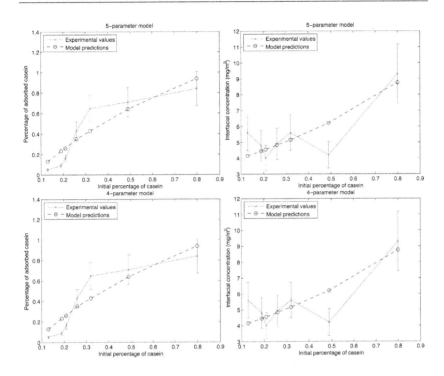

Figure 3.6. *Fitting for the two outputs of the casein model on the training set (database 1), with five parameters (top) and four parameters (bottom). The bars represent the measurement error in the experimental data. For a color version of this figure, see www.iste.co.uk/lutton/algorithms.zip*

The available data only characterize the emulsion at the initial and final states of the process; therefore, it is not possible for the model to catch the dynamic of the process, while it provides accurate results for the final state of the emulsion. Consequently, we only focus on the asymptotic values of the solutions of system [3.2] or [3.3]. If we set a new timescale, $u = k_{cas}t$, and introduce the ratio between adsorption rates, $k = \frac{k_{wp}}{k_{cas}}$, system [3.3] is rewritten as follows:

$$\begin{cases}
\frac{dP}{du} = \frac{P}{S_0(P+1)} \left[kP(S_{f_{all}} + S_{f_{res}}) - S_{f_{all}} \right. \\
\qquad \left. \times \left(1 - \frac{(m_{cas_0} - m_{cas})s_{cas}}{S_0}\right)\right] \\
\frac{dm_{cas}}{du} = -\frac{S_{f_{all}} m_{cas}}{S_0(P+1)} \\
\qquad \times \left(1 - \frac{(m_{cas_0} - m_{cas})s_{cas}}{S_0}\right) \\
\frac{dS_{f_{all}}}{du} = -\frac{S_{f_{all}} m_{cas}}{S_0(P+1)} \left[ks_{wp}P^2 + s_{cas} \right. \\
\qquad \left. \times \left(1 - \frac{(m_{cas_0} - m_{cas})s_{cas}}{S_0}\right)\right] \\
\frac{dS_{f_{res}}}{du} = -\frac{m_{cas}}{S_0(P+1)} \left[ks_{wp}S_{f_{res}}P^2 - \alpha s_{cas}S_{f_{all}} \right. \\
\qquad \left. \times \left(1 - \frac{(m_{cas_0} - m_{cas})s_{cas}}{S_0}\right)\right]
\end{cases}$$

[3.4]

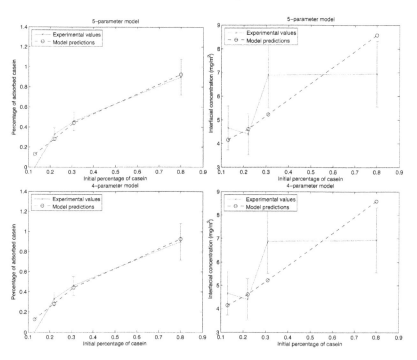

Figure 3.7. *Fitting for the two outputs of the casein model on the validation set (database 2), with five parameters (top) and four parameters (bottom). The bars represent the measurement error in the experimental data. For a color version of this figure, see www.iste.co.uk/lutton/algorithms.zip*

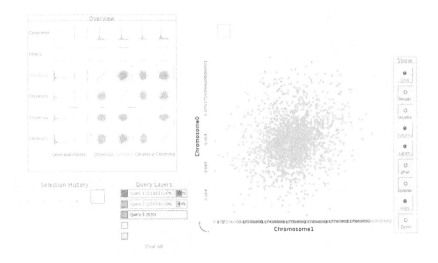

Figure 3.8. *Zoomed in view using GraphDice. Red points correspond to good fitness values, and yellow points to best fitness values. The optima values are concentrated on a point. For a color version of this figure, see www.iste.co.uk/lutton/algorithms.zip*

The change in timescale does not impact on the stationary states, which means that systems [3.3] and [3.4] lead to the same asymptotic values. Note also that only the $k = \frac{k_{wp}}{k_{cas}}$ ratio is involved in [3.4], which means that it is possible to express the asymptotic values only with respect to k. This result is in accordance with the visual analysis presented above.

3.3. Conclusions

The coupling of evolutionary algorithms with visualization proves to be an efficient strategy for exploring a food model. For the milk gel model, it was possible to reduce the complexity of the model due to the nature of the available data. Experimental measurements did actually not give access to the temporal data: some parameters governing the dynamics were thus impossible to define in a unique way, and using a ratio was enough to fit the model to the data.

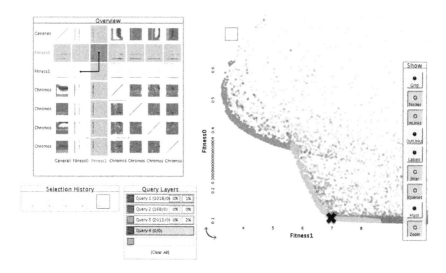

Figure 3.9. *The Pareto front has been highlighted in three colors: red for the points where fitness1 dominates, green for the points where fitness0 dominates and yellow for balanced fitness area. The optimal point found with CMA-ES (four-parameter problem) is situated under the "X" mark. For a color version of this figure, see www.iste.co.uk/lutton/algorithms.zip*

This approach can be used to explore other models, including models that are not fully analytically defined. It has to be noted, however, that both the structure of the model and the nature of available data have a strong impact on the models that can be explored. For instance, if there are no data that make it possible to access dynamic behaviors, there is no way to instantiate dynamic parameters in a unique way. A way to address this issue might exploit interactions with human experts as an additional source of information. Further studies will consider the integration of expert knowledge by allowing the expert to interactively redesign the model, or inject uncertainty information for data sample points. Specific methods for dynamic models will also be considered.

3.4. Acknowledgments

The research leading to these results received funding from the European Community's Seventh Framework Programme (FP7/2007–2013) under grant agreement FP7-222 654-DREAM.

The authors would like to thank Romain Reuillon and Mathieu Leclaire for their help with Scala programming; Claire Surel and Marc Anton from INRA BIA Nantes, and Alan Mackie and Marine Rouland from IFR Norwich for their help in building of the model and providing experiments.

4

Interactive Model Learning

In this chapter, we present a study based on an evolutionary framework to explore what would be a reasonable compromise between interaction and automated optimization in finding possible solutions for a complex problem, namely the learning of Bayesian network (BN) structures, a non-deterministic (NP)-hard problem[1] between where user knowledge can be crucial to distinguish polynomial solutions of equal fitness but very different physical meaning. Even though several classes of complex problems can be effectively tackled with evolutionary computation, most possess qualities that are difficult to directly encode in the *fitness function* or in the individual's *genotype description*. Expert knowledge can sometimes be used to integrate the missing information, but new challenges arise when searching for the best way to access it: full human interaction can lead to user-fatigue, while a completely automated evolutionary process can miss important contributions by the expert. For our study, we developed a graphical user interface (GUI)-based prototype application that lets an expert user guide the evolution of a network by alternating between fully interactive and completely automatic steps. Preliminary user tests were able to show that despite still requiring some improvements with regard to its efficiency, the proposed approach achieves its goal of delivering satisfying results for an expert user in food model case studies. The

---

1 https://en.wikipedia.org/wiki/NP-hardness.

work described in this chapter was done with André Spritzer and published in [TON 13b].

4.1. Introduction

Efficiently using algorithmic solvers to address real-world problems initially requires us to deal with the difficult issue of designing an adequate optimization landscape – i.e. defining the search space and the function to be optimized. The Bayesian Network Structure Learning (BNSL) problem is a good example of a complex optimization task in which expert knowledge is of crucial importance in the formulation of the problem, being as essential as the availability of a large enough experimental dataset. By its very nature, BNSL is also at least bi-objective: its aim is to optimize the designing of a model to the data while keeping its complexity low. The balance between the multiple objectives has to be decided by an expert user, either before or after, depending on whether a mono- or multiobjective solver is used. Other high-level design choices made by the expert condition the type of model that is searched (i.e. the definition of the search space) and the constraints that are applied to the search.

Lack of experimental data is a common issue in real-world instances of the BNSL problem, making the optimization task multimodal or even badly conditioned. Although previous work has proven that evolutionary algorithm (EA) approaches tend to be more robust to data sparseness than other learning algorithms [TON 12], an efficient and versatile way of collecting expert knowledge still represents important progress. Interaction with the expert, for instance, can be useful to disambiguate solutions considered equivalent, given the available dataset. How to best access an expert's knowledge, however, is still an open issue: asking a human user for input at a high frequency may lead to user fatigue; not asking frequently enough might result in too little feedback. In this chapter, we present a study that constitutes a first step in reaching this balance between interaction and automation.

For our study, we developed a prototype application that allows an expert user to guide the evolution of a BN. The prototype works by alternating steps of interactive visualization with fully automated evolution. The original network and evolved solutions are always displayed to the user as interactive node-link diagrams through which constraints can be added so that the function to be optimized can be refined. Our approach is related to humanized computation as defined by [FR 06] (EvoINTERACTION Workshops), i.e. "systems where human and computational intelligence cooperate".

The use of interactive evolution algorithms (IEAs or IEC) is the most common approach for humanized computation. This strategy considers the user as the provider of a fitness function (or as a part of it) inside an evolutionary loop and has been applied to various domains, such as art, industrial design, the tuning of ear implants and data retrieval [TAK 08, SIM 08]. There are, however, different ways to interlace human interaction and optimization computations that may be as simple as what we study in this chapter (i.e. an iterative scheme) or as sophisticated as collaborative learning and problem-solving using Serious Games or Crowd Sourcing [BEL 09, VOU 11, POT 10]. An interesting feature of these latter approaches is that they consider various tools to deal with what they call "user engagement", which may represent a new source of inspiration to address the issue of "user fatigue" with IEAs.

This chapter is organized as follows. Section 4.2 gives a short background on BNs and how they can be visualized, as well as on methods used for dealing with the BNSL problem. Section 4.3 details our proposed approach. Experimental results are presented in section 4.4 and an analysis is detailed in section 4.5. Finally, our conclusions and some possible directions for future research are discussed in section 4.6.

4.2. Background

4.2.1. *Bayesian networks*

Formally, a BN is a directed acyclic graph whose nodes represent variables and whose arcs encode conditional dependencies between the variables. This graph is called the *structure* of the network and the nodes containing probabilistic information are called the *parameters* of the network. Figure 4.1 shows an example of a BN.

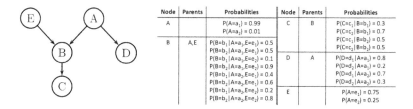

Figure 4.1. *Left: a directed acyclic graph. Right: the parameters it is associated with. Together they form a Bayesian network, BN, whose joint probability distribution is*

$$P(BN) = P(A)P(B|A, E)P(C|B)P(D|A)P(E)$$

The set of parent nodes of a node X_i is denoted by $pa(X_i)$. In a BN, the joint probability distribution of the node values can be written as the product of the local probability distribution of each node and its parents:

$$P(X_1, X_2, ..., X_n) = \prod_{i=1}^{n} P(X_i|pa(X_i))$$

4.2.2. *The structure learning problem*

Learning the optimal structure of a BN starting from a dataset is a NP-hard problem [CHI 94]. Even obtaining good approximations is extremely difficult, since compromises between the representativeness of the model and its complexity must be found. The algorithmic approaches devised to solve this problem can be split into heuristic algorithms (which often rely upon statistical considerations on the learning set) and score and search meta-heuristics. Recently, hybrid techniques have produced promising results.

Heuristic algorithms: the machine-learning community uses several state-of-the-art heuristics algorithms to build BN structures from data.

Some of them rely upon the evaluation of conditional independence between variables, while others are similar to score- and-search approaches, only performed in a local area of the solutions' space, determined through heuristic considerations. The main strength of these techniques is their ability to return high-quality results in a time that is negligible when compared to meta-heuristics.

Two of the best algorithms in this category are *greedy thick thinning* (GTT) [CHE 97] and *Bayesian search* (BS) [COO 92]. Although a detailed description of the two procedures is outside the scope of this work, it is important to highlight the most relevant difference between them. While GTT is fully deterministic, always returning the same solution for the same input, BS is stochastic, starting from different random positions at each execution. Both GTT and BS implementations can be found in commercial products such as GeNie/SMILE [DRU 99].

Evolutionary approaches: among score- and-search meta-heuristics, EAs are prominently featured. Several attempts to tackle the problem have been tested, ranging from evolutionary programming [WON 99], to cooperative co-evolution [BAR 09] and island models [REG 12]. Interestingly, some of the evolutionary approaches to BNSL in the literature show features of memetic algorithms, hinting that injecting expert knowledge might be necessary to obtain good results on such a complex problem. For example, [WON 99] employs a *knowledge-guided mutation* that performs a local search to find the most interesting arc to add or remove. In [DEL 07], a local search is used to select the best way to break a loop in a non-valid individual. The K2GA algorithm [LAR 96a], in its turn, exploits a genetic algorithm to navigate the space of possible node orderings, and then runs the greedy local optimization K2, which quickly converges on good structures starting from a given sorting of the variables in the problem.

Memetic algorithms: these are "population-based meta-heuristics composed of an evolutionary framework and a set of local search algorithms which are activated within the generation cycle of the external framework" [HAR 05]. First presented in [NOR 91], they have gained in popularity in the last few years [NER 12]. What makes these stochastic optimization techniques attractive is their ability to quickly find high-quality results while still maintaining the exploration potential of a classic EA. Their effectiveness has been proven in several real-world problems [FAN 07, NGU 09] and there have been initial attempts to employ them in the structure learning problem. In particular, in [TON 13a] the authors combine the exploratory power of an EA with the efficient exploitation of GTT, obtaining BN structures with higher representation and lower complexity than results produced by the most prominently featured heuristic methods.

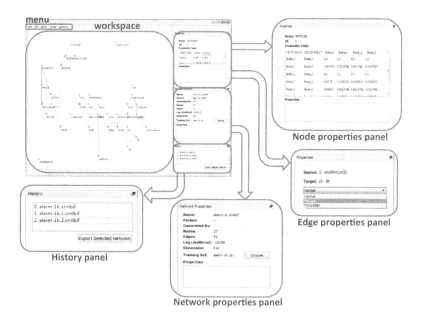

Figure 4.2. *Overview of the prototype's interface in use: a network being displayed and prepared for evolution. Node properties panel: the table shows the parameters or, in other words, the conditional probabilities for the corresponding variable. Edge properties panel: the arcs can be set as forced or forbidden before running the structure learning algorithms. Network properties panel: the log-likelihood expresses how well the current network expresses the dataset, while the dimension is a measure of the network's complexity. History panel: every time a structure learning algorithm is run, a new network is added to the history*

4.2.3. *Visualizing BNs*

It has been shown that efficient interactions in humanized computation require efficient visualizations [HAY 00]. Current visualization tools for BNs rely on classical graph layouts for the qualitative part of the BN, i.e. its graphical structure. A difficult issue remains regarding the quantitative part of the BN: the conditional probability set associated with each node of the graph. It was noted in 2005 that "the work performed on causal relation visualization has been surprisingly low" [CHI 05]. Various solutions have been proposed, as in [COS 11], BayViz [CHI 05, COS 11] SMILE and GeNIe [DRU 99] or VisualBayes [WIL 06]. To our knowledge, the most advanced and versatile visualization interface for dealing with structure learning is GeNIe, a development environment for building graphical decision-theoretic models from the Decision Systems Laboratory of the University of Pittsburgh: it has gained a notoriety in teaching, research and industry.

None of these tools, however, has really been designed to run a smooth interaction scheme and to easily allow users to revisit the learning stage after the visualization. Our approach explores new features for visualization-based interactive structure learning strategies. It does not currently address quantitative visualization, though that may be considered in the future.

4.3. Proposed approach

Automated structure learning processes usually score candidate networks with specific metrics; however, networks with similar scores might be extremely different from a user's point of view. In order to take into account human expertise, we propose an interactive evolutionary tool for BNSL.

To perform our study, a prototype application has been developed through which users can control the generation and evolution of the BN. This application consists of a GUI (Figure 4.2) that serves as a hub for network manipulation and interactive evolution. The GUI consists of the *menu*, the *workspace*, a *node/edge properties panel*, a *network properties panel* and a *history panel*.

To start the process from scratch, users can load a .csv file containing a training set by selecting the appropriate option from the prototype's *File* menu. Alternatively, users can load an already computed network from an XMLBIF file by choosing the corresponding option from the same menu. Once a network is loaded, it will be displayed as a node-link diagram on the workspace, with nodes represented as labeled circles and edges as directed line segments. When a network is first loaded, nodes are arranged in a circular layout. Other layout options can be found in the *Layout* menu, and include the layouts of Gürsoy-Atun [GÜR 00], Fruchterman-Reingold [FRU 91] and Sugiyama [SUG 81] (see Figure 4.3).

Figure 4.3. *Sample of layout options, from left to right: circular, Gürsoy-Atun, Fruchterman-Reingold and Sugiyama layouts of the Alarm BN benchmark*

Navigation in the workspace consists of zooming and panning. Users can zoom in or out by spinning the mouse wheel and pan using the scrollbars that appear when the visualization is too big to fit in the workspace's view. Panning can also be performed with the *drag tool*, accessible from the *Edit* menu. When this tool is active, panning can be performed by clicking and dragging anywhere on the workspace.

By default, when a network is first loaded the *selection tool* is active. This tool allows users to select nodes and edges and move them around the workspace by clicking and dragging. Multiple objects can be selected by clicking on each object separately while the *Ctrl* key is pressed or by clicking on an empty area of the workspace and dragging so that the shown selected area intersects with or covers the desired objects. Clicking and dragging on any selected object will move all others along with it.

Users can connect nodes to one another with the *Create Edge* tool, available from the *Graph* menu. Once this tool is active, the new edge can be created by first clicking on the desired origin node and subsequently on the target one. While the new edge is being created, a dashed line is shown from the origin node to the current cursor position to help users keep track of the operation. If, after choosing the origin node, they click on empty space instead of on another node, the edge creation is cancelled. To delete an edge from the graph, after selecting it they can either press the *Delete* key on the keyboard or select *Remove Edge* from the *Graph* menu. This operation is irreversible so a dialogue box will pop up to ask for their confirmation.

When an object is selected in the workspace, its properties are displayed in the properties panel (node properties and edge properties panels in Figure 4.2). Node properties include its name and numeric ID in the graph as well as its probability table (if a training set has been loaded) and a list of other properties that might be present in the network's corresponding file. Edge properties show the ID and name of an edge's origin and target nodes and helps users prepare the network for evolution by setting the edge as *forced* or *forbidden*, or leaving it as a normal edge. Forced edges will appear in green in the workspace, while forbidden edges will appear in red.

From the moment the network is loaded, its properties are displayed in the network properties panel (Figure 4.2). These properties include the number of nodes and edges, the network's log likelihood and dimension, and other properties loaded from the network file, all updated every time there is a change in the graph. If the network was generated by evolving another, the parent network and the method used to generate it will also be shown. The training set that will be used to evolve the network can also be set from within this panel through the corresponding field's *Choose* button, which lets users load a .csv file. Note that the training set must be compatible with the network (i.e. have the exact same nodes).

If the current network has been created directly from a training set or one has been loaded in the network properties panel, it can be evolved into new networks. This is done through the learning algorithms accessible through the *Learning* menu. Users can choose from three techniques: GTT, BS and μGP. When one is chosen, its corresponding configuration dialog is shown, where parameters for the evolution can be set and, for the case of μGP, stop conditions defined.

After evolution, the workspace is updated to display the new network. The new network is also added to the list in the history panel (Figure 4.2). In this panel, the current network is always highlighted. Users can change the currently displayed network by clicking on its name and export it to an XMLBIF file through the *Export selected network* button. The latest layout is always kept when alternating between the different networks.

The prototype application was implemented in C++ using the Qt 4.8.2 framework and the Boost (http://www.boost.org) and OGDF [CHI 12] libraries. Figure 4.2 shows the prototype in use. A couple of networks have been generated using the learning algorithms, with the one displayed on the workspace having been created with GTT. The user has set some of the edges to forced (MINVOLSET to VENTMACH and MINVOLSET to DISCONNECT) and forbidden (INTUBATION to SHUNT) and a node has been selected (DISCONNECT).

4.4. Experimental setup

In order to validate the proposed approach, test runs were performed in cooperation with two experts on food processing and agriculture. Agrifood research lines exploit BN models to represent complex industrial processes for food production.

The first expert (Cédric Baudrit) analyzed a dataset on cheese ripening [BAU 10]. It consists of 27 variables evaluating different properties of the cheese from the point of view of the producer. Of these variables, seven are qualitative while the other 20 refer to chemical processes. A candidate solution for the dataset is reported in Figure 4.4.

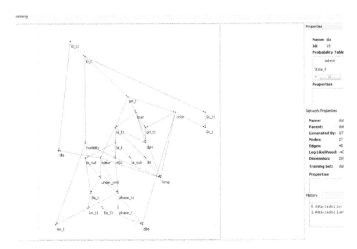

Figure 4.4. *A sample configuration of the complete network used in the test trial. The Sugyiama layout was preferred by the expert to visualize the structure*

The second expert (Nathalie Perrot) analyzed a dataset on biscuit baking. It consists of 10 variables describing properties of the biscuits, such as weight and color, and controlling variables of the process, such as heat in the top and bottom parts of the oven.

After a preliminary run, the setup of the memetic algorithm was changed in order to better fit the user's preferences. Since the prototype was not optimized with regard to the running speed of the evolutionary process, the population size was reduced in comparison to the parameters reported in [TON 12] so that a compromise could be reached between the quality of the results and time the user needed to wait before seeing the outcome.

4.5. Analysis and perspectives

The expert users' responses to the prototype's graphical user interface were generally positive. The ease of arc manipulation, which made it possible to immediately see improvements in the network's representativeness and/or dimension, was well received. Also commended were the automatic layout algorithms, which were extensively used when considering the entire network. The possibility of rapidly browsing through the history of networks was used thoroughly by the experts and found to be advantageous. They felt, however, that comparing candidates would have been more immediate and effective if the interface allowed such candidates to be shown side-by-side, two at a time.

Since the process of structure learning is interactive, the users also noted how the possibility of cumulating constraints would be beneficial. In the current framework, the forced and forbidden arcs are clearly visible in each network, but they have to be set again every time a learning method is run. Despite results of slightly higher quality provided by the memetic approach, both users felt that the improvement in quality did not justify the extra time needed to obtain the solution (this approach can take up to several minutes, while the others finish running after a few seconds). For this reason, the experts favored a more interactive approach, running the deterministic heuristic (GTT), changing the forced and forbidden arcs in its results and repeating the process until a satisfactory solution was found.

Concerning algorithm performance, in order to understand the efficacy of the tool, one of the users repeatedly divided the original network into smaller networks, being more confident that in this way he/she could highlight links that he/she deemed right or wrong (see Figure 4.5 for an example). In networks with a reduced number of variables, however, the difference in performance between the methods became less clear, since smaller search spaces inevitably favors the heuristics. Nevertheless, the second expert was able to use the tool to eventually exclude a potential relationship between two variables in the process by iteratively generating configurations and then focusing on the log-likelihood values presented by the different candidate solutions.

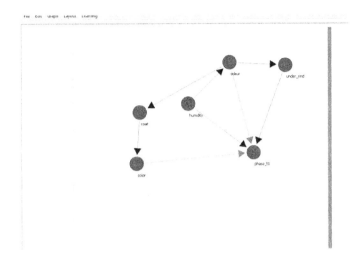

Figure 4.5. *One of the subnetworks extensively explored by the user. In particular, this one contains only qualitative variables from the original dataset. For a color version of this figure, see www.iste.co.uk/lutton/algorithms.zip*

In summary, the feedback given by the expert user in this first trial allowed us to compile a list of features that should make the structure learning experience more efficient:

1) speeding up the memetic algorithm was recommended, and could be done straightforwardly by using parallel evaluations and letting the user tweak some internal parameters;

2) allowing the user to compare solutions side-by-side could be very helpful for the user, since humans are more inclined to visually compare two networks at the same time than by simply browsing through the history;

3) modifying the memetic algorithm to ask for the user's input at predetermined points (in order to try to extract his or her preferences by comparing networks, as in user-centric memetic algorithms [ESP 12]) might be a way to involve the user in a more time-consuming evolutionary process;

4) designing special features to address dynamic Bayesian networks (DBNs). DBNs are extensively used in the agrifood field, and

existing BN tools are often missing an inference and learning method specifically tailored for these structures;

5) minor features, such as allowing the user to reverse arcs, visualizing node-related statistics in pop-up windows (for clarity), selecting several arcs at the same time and making it possible to select only a subset of variables from the original dataset.

4.6. Conclusion

In this chapter, we presented a preliminary study on balancing automatic evolution and user interaction for the NP-hard problem of BNSL. The study was performed through a graphical user interface.

A test run with input from modeling experts showed that the tool is able to assist the user in expressing knowledge that would be difficult to encode in a classical fitness function, returning more satisfying models than a completely automatic approach. Despite the promising preliminary results, several improvements must be performed on the proposed framework to enhance usability and progress toward an optimal balance between the automatic evolution of results and user interaction. For example, the evolutionary approach included at the core of the framework was found to be too time consuming when compared to fast state-of-the-art heuristic algorithms.

Further developments will add other evolutionary structure learning algorithms, as well as the possibility for more user interaction in the definition of parameters and during the evolution itself.

Modeling Human Expertise Using Genetic Programming

Co-operative–co-evolution techniques (CCEAs, also called "Parisian" approaches) actually allow us to represent the searched solution as an aggregation of several individuals (or even as a whole population), as each individual only bears a part of the solution searched. This scheme allows us to use artificial Darwinism principles in a more economic way, and the gain in terms of robustness and efficiency is important. In this chapter, we present two experiments related to the modeling of an industrial agrifood process, where cooperative–co-evolution techniques have proven successful. Experiments have focused on a specific problem: the modeling of a Camembert cheese ripening process. Two related complex optimization problems have been considered:

– a deterministic modeling problem, the phase prediction problem for which a search for a closed form tree expression has been performed using genetic programming (GP). This part of the study has been performed in collaboration with Olivier Barrière, Cédric Baudrit, Mariette Sicard and Bruno Pinaud;

– a Bayesian network (BN) structure estimation problem, considered as a two-stage problem, i.e. searching first for an approximation of an independence model (IM) using evolutionary algorithms (EAs), and then deducing, via a deterministic algorithm, a BN that represents the equivalence class of the IM found at the first stage. This part of the study was performed in collaboration with Olivier Barrière and Pierre-Henri Wuillemin[1].

5.1. Cooperative co-evolution

Cooperative co-evolution strategies rely on a formulation of the problem to be solved as a cooperative task, where individuals collaborate or compete in order to build a solution (see also section 2.6.2). They mimic the ability of natural populations to build solutions via a collective process. These techniques are used with success on various problems [DEJ 07, WIE 06], including learning problems [BON 05].

The large majority of these approaches deals with a co-evolution process that happens between a fixed number of separated populations [PAN 06, BUC 05, POP 06]. Here we study a different implementation of cooperative co-evolution principles, the Parisian approach [COL 00, OCH 08] described in Figure 5.1, that use cooperation mechanisms within a *single* population. It is based on a two-level representation of an optimization problem, in the sense that an individual of a Parisian population represents only a part of the solution to the problem. An aggregation of multiple individuals must be built in order to obtain a solution to the problem. In this way, the co-evolution of the whole population (or a major part of it) is favored instead of the emergence of a single best individual, as in classical evolutionary schemes. The motivation is to make a more efficient use of the genetic search process, and reduce the computational expense. Successful applications of such a scheme usually rely on a lower cost evaluation of the partial solutions (i.e. the individuals of the population), while computing the full evaluation only once at each generation.

---

1 LIP6-CNRS UMR7606, 75016 Paris.

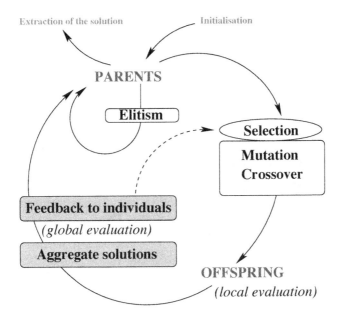

Figure 5.1. *A Parisian EA: a single-population cooperative–co-evolution. For a color version of this figure, see www.iste.co.uk/lutton/algorithms.zip*

5.2. Modeling agrifood industrial processes

The study we present below is part of the French INCALIN research project[2], whose goal is the modeling of agrifood industrial processes. In such food industries, manufacturing processes consist of successive operations whose underlying mechanisms are sometimes still ill-known, such as the cheese ripening process. The challenge of INCALIN is understanding the causal relationships between ingredients and physicochemical or microbiological characteristics, and sensory and nutritional properties. The intriguing question is how microlevel properties determine or at least influence macrolevel properties?

2 Supported by the French ANR-PNRA fund.

Various macroscopic models have been explored to embed expert knowledge, such as expert systems [IOA 04a, IOA 04b, IOA 06], neural networks [JIM 05, NI 98], mechanistic models [ALD 06, RIA 07] and dynamic Bayesian networks (DBNs) [BAU 08].

The major problem common to these techniques is related to the sparseness of available data: collecting experimental data is a long and difficult process, and resulting datasets are often uncertain or even wrong. For example, a complete cheese ripening process last 40 days, and some tests are destructive, i.e a sample cheese is consumed in the analysis. Other measurements require us to grow bacteria in Petri dishes and then to count the number of colonies, which takes a lot of time. Therefore, the precision of the resulting model is often limited by the small number of valid experimental data, and parameter estimation procedures have to deal with incomplete, sparse and uncertain data.

5.2.1. *The Camembert cheese-ripening process*

Experimental procedures in laboratories ("model cheeses") use pasteurized milk inoculated with *Kluyveromyces marxianus*, *Geotrichum candidum*, *Penicillium camemberti* and *Brevibacterium auriantiacum* under aseptic conditions:

– *Kluyveromyces marxianus* is one of the key flora of Camembert cheese. One of its principal activities is the fermentation of lactose (noted lo) [CHO 97a, CHO 97b] (curd de-acidification by lactose consumption). Three dynamics are apparent in the timeline of *K. marxianus* growth [LEC 04, LEC 16]. First, there is an exponential growth during about 5 days that corresponds to a decrease in lactose concentration. Second, the concentration of *K. marxianus* remains constant during about 15 days. Third, the concentration decreases slowly.

– *Geotrichum candidum* plays a key role in ripening because it contributes to the development of flavor, taste and aroma of cheeses [ARF 03, BOU 05, LEN 84]. One of its principal activities is the consumption of lactate (noted la). Three dynamics are apparent in the timeline of *G. candidum* growth [LEC 04, LEC 16]. First, there is a latency period lasting about 3 days. Second, there is an exponential growth that corresponds to a decrease in lactate concentration, and thus an increase in pH. Third, the concentration, of *G. candidum* remains constant to the end of ripening.

During ripening, these soft-mold cheeses behave like an extremely complex (a bioreactor) to be modeled as a whole. Human expert operators have a decisive role. Relationships between microbiological and physicochemical changes depend on environmental conditions (e.g. temperature and relative humidity) [LEC 16] and influence the quality of the ripened cheeses [GRI 93, LEC 04]. A ripening expert is able to estimate the current state of some of the complex reactions at a macroscopic level through his or her perceptions (sight, touch, smell and taste). Control decisions are then generally based on these subjective but robust expert measurements. The subjective estimation of the current state of the ripening process, discretized in four phases is an important regulation parameter:

– *phase 1* is characterized by the evolution of surface humidity (drying process). At the beginning, the surface of the cheese is very wet and evolves until it presents a rather dry aspect. The cheese is white with fresh odor;

– *phase 2* begins with the apparition of a *P. camemberti* coat (i.e. the white coat at the surface of cheese), and it is characterized by first change in color and the development of a "mushroom" odor;

– *phase 3* is characterized by the thickening of the creamy underrind. Light brown *P. camemberti* cover the surface of the cheese;

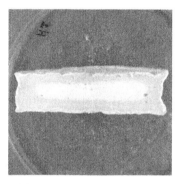

– *phase 4* is defined by strong ammoniac odor and the dark brown aspect of the rind.

These four steps are representative of the main evolution of the cheese during ripening. The expert's knowledge is obviously not limited to these four phases, but these phases help to evaluate the whole dynamics of ripening and to detect drift from the standard evolution.

5.2.2. *Modeling expertise on cheese ripening*

A major problem addressed in the INCALIN project is the search for automatic procedures that mimic the way human experts aggregate data through their senses to estimate and regulate the ripening of the cheese.

In this work, we explore how GP and cooperative–co-evolution algorithms (CCEAs) can be used to capture (learn) expert knowledge. Section 5.3 deals with the estimation of the phase using GP and section 5.4 addresses the problem of learning the structure of a BN, with an approach based on IMs.

5.3. Phase estimation using GP

In a previous work on cheese-ripening modeling [BAU 08, PIN 08], a DBN (Figure 5.2) has been built, using human expert knowledge, to represent the macroscopic dynamic of each variable. The phase the network is in at time t plays a determinant role in the prediction of the variables at time $t + 1$. Moreover, four relevant variables have been identified, the derivative of pH, la, $K.$ $marxianus$ and $B.$ $auriantiacum$ at time t, allowing the model to predict the phase at time $t + 1$. This leads to a computer-based phase estimation to model the way experts aggregate information from their senses.

5.3.1. *Phase estimation using a classical GP*

A GP approach is used to search for a convenient formula that links the four derivatives of microorganisms' proportions to the phase at each time step t (static model), without prior knowledge of the phase at $t - 1$.

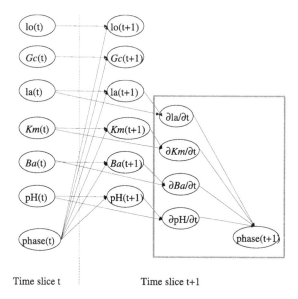

Figure 5.2. *DBN representing the dynamics of variables depending on the observation of ripening phases. The static BN used for comparison in the sequel is in the box on the right*

This problem is a symbolic regression one; however, it has to be noted that the small number of samples and their irregular distribution make it difficult. Results will be compared with the performances of a static BN, extracted from the DBN [BAU 08] (the part within the box in Figure 5.2), and with very simple learning algorithms (multilinear prediction, see section 5.3.2.5).

5.3.1.1. *Search space*

The derivatives of four variables will be considered, namely the derivative of pH (acidity), la (lactose proportion), and *K. marxianus* and *B. auriantiacum* (lactic acid bacteria proportions, see section 5.2.1), for the estimation of the phase (static problem). The GP will search for a phase estimator $\widehat{Phase}(t)$, i.e. a function defined as follows:

$$\widehat{Phase}(t) = f\left(\frac{\partial pH}{\partial t}, \frac{\partial la}{\partial t}, \frac{\partial Km}{\partial t}, \frac{\partial Ba}{\partial t}\right)$$

The function set is made up of arithmetic operators: $\{+, -, *, /, \hat{\ }, log\}$, with protected $/$ and log, and logical operators $\{if, >, <, =, and, or, xor, not\}$ in order to allow a complex estimation formula.

The terminal set is made up of the four partial derivatives plus real constants. The constant's values are not limited, but randomly initialized using one of the following laws, $\mathcal{U}$ $[0, 1]$, $-\mathcal{U}$ $[0, 1]$, $\mathcal{N}$ $(0, 1)$, also randomly chosen. ($\mathcal{U}$ is the uniform law, and $\mathcal{N}$ the normal law.)

5.3.1.2. *Fitness function*

Available data are shared in two sets a learning set and a test set, that are randomly chosen within the available dataset for each run. The 16 available experiments are thus randomly shared between learning and test sets. The size of the learning sets vary from 10 to 15 experiments, while the size of the corresponding tests set vary from one to six experiments (see section 5.3.2.5).

The fitness function, *to be minimized*, is made up of a factor that measures the quality of the fitting on the learning set, plus a "parsimony" penalization factor in order to minimize the size (number of nodes) of the evolved structures (to avoid bloat). It is divided by the number of variables involved in the evaluated tree in order to favor structures that embed all four variables of the problem (this is a requirement of biologists; experiments also show that recognition results are better with this constraint):

$$fitness = \frac{\sum\limits_{learning\_set} \left| f\left(\frac{\partial pH}{\partial t}, \frac{\partial la}{\partial t}, \frac{\partial Km}{\partial t}, \frac{\partial Ba}{\partial t}\right) - Phase(t)\right| + W \#Nodes}{\#Variables + 1}$$

The parameter W has been experimentally tuned, and the optimal value ($W = 1$) favors evolution of structures with 30–40 nodes.

5.3.1.3. *Genetic operators*

A classical tree crossover (exchange of subtrees from a randomly chosen node) has been used with probability p_c (defined per tree), as a means of evolving the structure of the tree. Two types of mutations have been used:

– a *subtree mutation* (mutation of the structure) that randomly rebuilds a new subtree from a randomly chosen node, applied with probability p_{sm} (defined per tree);

– a *point mutation* (mutation of node content) applied with probability p_{cm} (also defined per tree) that does not modify the structure, but randomly changes the content of each node of the tree within the set of compatible functions or terminals (arity constraints). The probabilities (defined per node) are detailed in Table 5.1. Real values are considered separately and undergo a real mutation with probability p_{rm} as a multiplicative perturbation according to a χ^2 law of parameter N:

$$x' = x \frac{\sum_{i=1}^{N} \mathcal{N}(0,1)^2}{N}$$

p_{rm} and N vary linearly according to generations, from 0.1 to 0.5 for p_{rm}, and from 1 to 1000 for N, in order to start with rather infrequent large radius mutations and finish with more frequent mutations with smaller radius.

From	to	Probability
Operator	Operator	0.1
Variable	Variable	0.1
Variable	Constant	0.05
Constant	Variable	0.05
Constant	Constant	p_{rm}: 0.1 to 0.5
		N: 1 to 1000

Table 5.1. *Probabilities of point mutation operators*

Crossover, subtree and point mutation probabilities vary along evolution according to the adapting scheme [DAV 89] available in the GPLAB toolbox [SIL 05]. p_c, p_{sm} and pcm are initially fixed to $\frac{1}{3}$, and are updated according statistics of success of the various operators computed on a tuneable window of past generations.

5.3.2. *Phase estimation using a Parisian GP*

Instead of searching for a phase estimator as a single monolithic function, phase estimation can actually be split into four combined (and simpler) phase-detection trees as shown in Figure 5.3. The structures searched are binary output functions (or binarized functions) that characterize one of the four phases. The population is then split into four classes such that individuals of class k are good at characterizing phase k. Finally, a global solution is made up of at least one individual of each class in order to be able to classify the sample into one of the four previous phases via a voting scheme detailed at the end of this section.

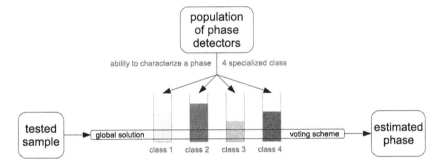

Figure 5.3. *Phase estimation using a Parisian GP. Four classes of phase detectors are defined: individuals of class k are good at characterizing phase k. For a color version of this figure, see www.iste.co.uk/lutton/algorithms.zip*

5.3.2.1. *Search space*

We now search for formulas of type: $I\left(\frac{\partial pH}{\partial t}, \frac{\partial la}{\partial t}, \frac{\partial Km}{\partial t}, \frac{\partial Ba}{\partial t}\right)$ with real outputs mapped to binary outputs, via a sign filtering: $(I() > 0) \to 1$ and $(I() \leq 0) \to 0$. The functions (except logical ones) and terminal sets, as well as the genetic operators, are the same as in the global approach above.

Using the available samples of the learning set, four real values can be computed in order to measure the capability of an individual I to characterize each phase:

$$k \in \{1, 2, 3, 4\} \quad F_k(I) =$$
$$3 \sum_{i,phase=k} \frac{I(sample(i))}{\#Samples_{phase=k}} - \sum_{i,phase \neq k} \frac{I(sample(i))}{\#Samples_{phase \neq k}}$$

i.e. if I is good for representing phase k, then $F_k(I) > 0$ and $F_{\neq k}(I) < 0$.

5.3.2.2. Local fitness

The local adjusted fitness value, *to be maximized*, is a combination of three factors:

$$AdjFit =$$
$$\max\{F_1, F_2, F_3, F_4\} \times \frac{\#Ind}{\#IndPhaseMax} \times \frac{NbMaxNodes}{NbNodes} \bigg| \text{ if } NbNodes > NbMaxNodes$$

The first factor is aimed at characterizing whether individual I is able to distinguish one of the four phases. The second factor tends to balance the individuals between the four phases ($\#IndPhaseMax$ is the number of individuals representing the phase corresponding to the $argmax$ of the first factor and $\#Ind$ is the total number of different individuals in the population). The third factor is a parsimony factor in order to avoid large structures. $NbMaxNodes$ has been experimentally tuned, and is currently fixed at 15.

Several fitness measures are used to rate individuals, namely *rawfitness*, i.e. the set of four values $\{F_1, F_2, F_3, F_4\}$ that measure the ability of the individual to characterize each phase, the *localfitness* = $\max(rawfitness)$, which represents the best characterized phase, and the adjusted fitness $adjfitness = \frac{localfitness}{\mu} \times \frac{\#IndPhaseMax}{\#Ind} \times \frac{\#NodesMax}{\#Nodes} \times bonus^\alpha$, which includes sharing, balance, parsimony and global fitness bonus terms.

5.3.2.3. Sharing distance

The set of measurements $\{F_1, F_2, F_3, F_4\}$ provides a simplified representation in $\mathbb{R}^4$ of the discriminant capabilities of each individual.

As the aim of a Parisian evolution is to evolve distinct subpopulations, each being adapted to one of the four subtasks (i.e. characterize one of the four phases), it is natural to use an Euclidean distance in this four-dimensional phenotype space as a basis of a simple fitness sharing scheme [DEB 89].

5.3.2.4. *Aggregation of partial solutions and global fitness*

At each generation, the population is distributed across four classes corresponding to the phase each individual characterizes best (i.e. the argmax of $\max\{F_1, F_2, F_3, F_4\}$ for each individual). The best 5% of each class are used via a voting scheme to decide the phase of each sample tested[3] (see Figure 5.3). The global fitness measures the proportion of correctly classified samples on the learning set:

$$GlobalFit = \frac{\sum\limits_{learning\_set} CorrectEstimations}{\#Samples}$$

The global fitness is then distributed as a multiplicative bonus on the individuals who participated in the vote:

$$LocalFit' = LocalFit \times (GlobalFit + 0.5)^{\alpha}.$$

As $GlobalFit \in [0, 1]$, multiplying by $(GlobalFit + 0.5) > 1$ corresponds to a bonus. Parameter α varies over generations. For the first generations (one-third of the total number of generations) $\alpha = 0$ (no bonus), and then α linearly increases from 0.1 to 1, in order to help the population to focus on the four peaks of the search space.

Two sets of indicators are computed at each generation (see section 5.3.2.5, third line in Figure 5.5):

– the sizes of each class, that show whether each phase is equally characterized by the individuals of the population;

– the discrimination capability of each phase, computed based on the best 5% individuals of each class as the minimum of:

---

3 This scheme may also yield the confidence level of the estimation. This measurement has not yet been exploited but can be used in future developments of the method.

$$\Delta = \max_{i \in [1,2,3,4]} \{F_i\} - \frac{\sum_{k \neq argmax\{F_i\}} \{F_k\}}{3} \qquad [5.1]$$

5.3.2.5. *Experimental analysis*

Available data have been collected from 16 experiments lasting 40 days, yielding 575 valid measurements[4]. The derivatives of pH, la, $K.$ *marxianus* and *B. auriantiacum* have been averaged and interpolated (spline interpolation) for some missing days. Logarithms of these quantities are considered.

The parameters of both GP methods are detailed in Table 5.2. The code has been developed in Matlab, using the GPLAB toolbox [SIL 05]. Comparative results of the four methods considered (multilinear regression, BN, GP and Parisian GP) are displayed in Figure 5.4, and a typical GP run is analyzed in Figure 5.5.

	GP	Parisian GP
Population size	1000	1000
Number of generations	100	50
Function set	arithmetic and logical functions	arithmetic functions only
Sharing	no sharing	$\sigma_{share} = 1$ at the beginning, then linear decrease from 1 to 0.1 $\alpha_{share} = 1$ (constant)

Table 5.2. *Parameters of the GP methods*

The multilinear regression algorithm used for comparison works as follows: the data are modeled as a linear combination of the four variables:

$$\widehat{Phase}(t) = \beta_1 + \beta_2 \frac{\partial pH}{\partial t} + \beta_3 \frac{\partial la}{\partial t} + \beta_4 \frac{\partial Km}{\partial t} + \beta_5 \frac{\partial Ba}{\partial t}$$

---

4 The data samples are relatively balanced except for phase 3, which has a longer duration, and thus a larger number of samples: we got 57 representatives of phase 1, 78 of phase 2, 247 of phase 3 and 93 of phase 4.

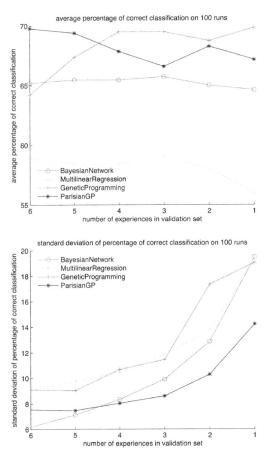

Figure 5.4. *Average (top) and standard-deviation (bottom) of recognition percentage on 100 runs for the four methods tested. The abscissa represent the size of the test set. For a color version of this figure, see www.iste.co.uk/lutton/algorithms.zip*

The five coefficients $\{\beta_1, \ldots, \beta_5\}$ are estimated using a simple least-squares scheme.

Experiments show that both GPs outperform multilinear regression and BN approaches in terms of recognition rates. Additionally, the analysis of a typical GP run (Figure 5.5) shows that much simpler structures are evolved: The average size of evolved structures is around

30 nodes for the classical GP approach and between 10 and 15 for the Parisian GP.

It also has to be noted in Figure 5.5 that co-evolution is balanced between the four phases, even though the third phase is the most difficult to characterize (this is in accordance with human experts' judgment, for which this phase is also the most ambiguous).

The development of a cooperative–co-evolution GP scheme (Parisian evolution) is very attractive as it allows the evolution of a simpler structure over fewer generations, and yields results that are easier to interpret. Moreover, the computation time is almost equivalent between both methods presented (100 generations of a classical GP against 50 generations of a Parisian one as one "Parisian" generation necessitates more complex operations, all in all). We can expect a more favorable behavior of the Parisian scheme on more complex issues than the phase prediction problem, as the benefit of splitting the global solutions into smaller components may be higher and may yield computational shortcuts (see, for example, [COL 00]).

5.3.3. *Variable population size strategies in a Parisian GP*

5.3.3.1. *Stagnation problem*

Let us consider local and global levels:

– the adjusted fitness is used as a basis for selection, crossover and mutation operators associated with a first elitism mechanism, which keeps the four best individuals *of the current generation* (one per phase) based on non-adjusted fitness in the population;

– at the end of each generation, the global fitness is computed and reinjected in the population as a bonus, combined with a second elitism mechanism, which keeps the four individuals *of the generation that yielded the best global fitness*;

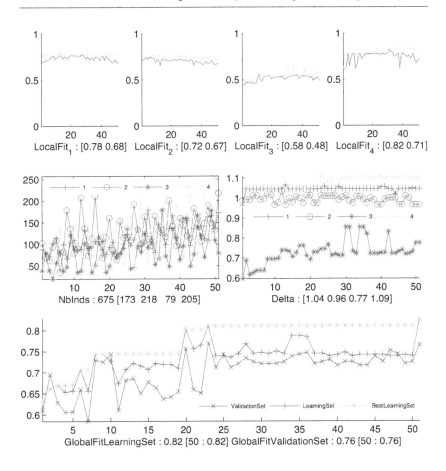

Figure 5.5. *A typical Parisian GP run. First line: the evolution with respect to generation number of the 5% best individuals for each phase. the upper curve of each of the four graphs is for the best individual. The lower curve is for the "worst of 5% best" individuals. Second line left: the distribution of individuals for each phase. The curves are very irregular but numbers of representatives of each phases are balanced. Second line right: Discrimination indicator Δ (equation 5.1), which shows that the third phase is the most difficult to characterize. Third line: evolution of the recognition rates of learning and test set. The best-so-far recognition rate on the learning set is tagged with a star. For a color version of this figure, see www.iste.co.uk/lutton/algorithms.zip*

Despite of local elitism and bonus mechanisms, global fitness is not a monotonically increasing function. A generation often notably improves the global fitness, while the generations that follow are not able to keep this fitness as we can see in Figure 5.6.

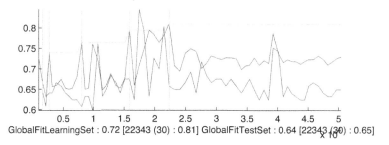

GlobalFitLearningSet : 0.72 [22343 (30) : 0.81] GlobalFitTestSet : 0.64 [22343 (30) : 0.65]

Figure 5.6. *Typical run of a Parisian GP: stagnation of global fitness.
For a color version of this figure, see
www.iste.co.uk/lutton/algorithms.zip*

To avoid this undesirable effect, a variable sized population Parisian GP strategy is explored, using adaptive deflating and inflating schemes for the population size. The idea is to group individuals with the same characteristics into "clusters" and remove the most useless ones at the end of every generation while periodically adding "fresh blood" to the population (i.e. new random individuals) if a stagnation criterion is fulfilled.

Various population sizing and resizing schemes have been studied in the literature for classical evolutionary schemes [LOB 05, EIB 04]. It has been clearly stated that adaptive population size allows us to build more efficient optimization algorithms by dynamically balancing the exploration and exploitation capabilities of the search, the gain in efficiency being measured in terms of number of fitness evaluations.

Common online population size adjustment schemes are related to the improvement of the best individual in the population, to the variance of population fitness, or rely on the notion of age and lifetime of individuals. There are also strategies based on competing subpopulations; for example, [SCH 96] proposed a scheme based on competing subpopulations: each subpopulation runs a different search strategy, and regularly compete with each other. The size of "good" strategies then increases while "bad" ones decreases, the sum of the sizes of all populations being constant.

However, to the best of our knowledge, there is no work on this type for cooperative–co-evolution scheme. The strategy we explore for single-population cooperative–co-evolution relies on the notion of improvement in global fitness, and allows us to allocate less local fitness evaluations to obtain a better result *in fine*. Tests have been performed in order to evaluate the improvements due to population deflation, then to population deflation plus inflation, in comparison to a constant population size scheme.

5.3.3.2. *Fair play comparison*

In order to fairly compare different schemes, results will be indexed with the number of new individuals' evaluations instead of the number of generations. As a result, for the same cost (i.e the same total number of evaluations) a decreasing-size population scheme "uses" more generations.

5.3.3.3. *Redundancy: diversity's hidden iceberg*

Because of the binarized output that only takes into account the sign of the identification function $I()$, several individuals may have the same raw fitness. This is often the case at the end of the evolution, which causes a loss of diversity.

5.3.3.4. *Clustering*

Individuals having the same $raw\,fitness$ are grouped into clusters. Then, inside each cluster, individuals are sorted according to their number of nodes, as described in Figure 5.7. The first and best one is the one with the smallest number of nodes.

5.3.3.5. *Elimination rules*

The elimination of useless individuals allows us to decrease the population size: an individual is considered as useless if it belongs to a big cluster and has a large number of nodes. The elimination rule depends on two parameters (to_keep and to_remove), in order to tune the decreasing speed of the population while keeping enough diversity.

The elimination procedure is called at the end of each generation. The detailed procedure is given in algorithm 1: if a cluster has fewer *to_keep* individuals, they are all kept: and if it has more, only the last *to_remove* individuals, having the largest number of nodes, are removed. Typical values of these parameters are $to\_keep = 7$ and $to\_remove = 1$.

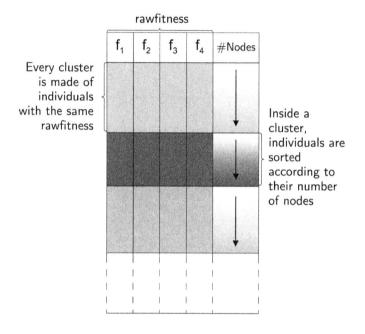

Figure 5.7. *Population clustering. For a color version of this figure, see www.iste.co.uk/lutton/algorithms.zip*

5.3.3.6. *Partial restart scheme*

In order to avoid stagnation due to over-specialization of the best individuals, we propose to periodically add "fresh blood" to the population (i.e. new random individuals) if a stagnation criterion is fulfilled. The corresponding algorithm uses one parameter denoted *to_insert*, typically set to a lower value than *to_keep* (see algorithm 2).

Algorithm 1: Elimination

Input: population of size N
Output: population of size lower or equal to N
foreach *cluster of the population* **do**
    if *size of the cluster greater than to_keep* **then**
        | remove the last *to_remove* individuals from the cluster
    else
        | keep all individuals from the cluster
    end
end

Algorithm 2: Partial restart

Input: population of size N
Output: population of size between N and N_{max}
creation of a fresh population of $N_{max} - N$ individuals randomly
created **foreach** *individual of the fresh population* **do**
    if *size of cluster in which the individual fits lower than*
    to_insert **then**
        | insert the individual into the corresponding cluster of the
        | old population
    end
end

In this way, if a cluster of the old population is empty or does not have enough elements according to a stricter rule than during the elimination process, it gets new elements. Moreover, the size of the subpopulation to be included being $N_{max} - N$, the final population is sure to be between N and N_{max}.

5.3.3.7. *Criterion of stagnation*

If the last improvement of the global fitness is older (in terms of generations) than the $stagnation\_threshold$, then the partial restart is triggered.

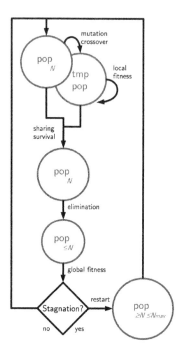

Figure 5.8. *Deflation–inflation scheme. For a color version of this figure, see www.iste.co.uk/lutton/algorithms.zip*

5.3.3.8. *Deflation–inflation scheme*

This scheme is made up of the following steps (see Figure 5.8):

– *mutations and crossover* yield a temporary population, $tmppop$;

– *local fitness* is computed on the temporary population, $localfitness(tmppop)$;

– *adjusted fitness* is computed via sharing, $sharing(pop+tmppop)$;

– *selection* of the N best individuals, $pop = survival(pop + tmppop)$;

– *elimination* of the useless individuals with algorithm 1, $pop = elimination(pop)$;

– *global fitness* computation of the global fitness of the population, $globalfitness(pop)$;

– *partial restart* if a stagnation criterion is met, using algorithm 2:
$pop = restart(pop)$.

5.3.3.9. *Typical runs*

Before introducing a complete statistical analysis, a preview of typical runs is given for each scheme, namely "fixed size" in Figure 5.9, "deflating only" in Figure 5.10 and "inflating + deflating" in Figure 5.11.

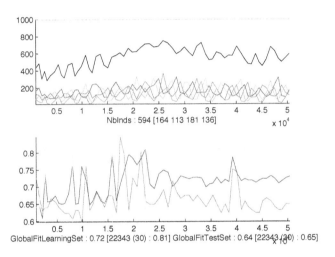

Figure 5.9. *Typical run of a Parisian GP (fixed-size scheme). Top: size of the population and number of distinct individuals in each class. Bottom: percentage of correct classification in the learning set and test sets. For a color version of this figure, see www.iste.co.uk/lutton/algorithms.zip*

When the size of the population is fixed, the total number of individuals is constant (here equal to 1,000), but we can see that inside this population the number of representatives of each class is quite balanced, and the number of distinct individuals is also quite stable. The drawback is that the global fitness is very irregular, and gets improvements only at the beginning of the evaluations and then stagnates.

With the deflating-only scheme, the population slowly decreases because we eliminate useless individuals. The number of distinct individuals gets close to the total number of individuals at the end of the evaluations. Nevertheless, there are still few improvements in the global fitness and stagnation is quickly reached.

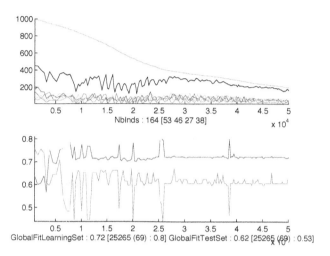

Figure 5.10. *Typical run of a Parisian GP (inflating + deflating). Top: size of the population and number of distinct individuals in each class. Bottom: percentage of correct classifications in the learning set and test sets. For a color version of this figure, see www.iste.co.uk/lutton/algorithms.zip*

On the contrary, with the deflating + inflating scheme, there are much greater improvements in the global fitness. The final recognition rate on the learning set is better than with the two other schemes. As far as the size of the population is concerned, we can observe the cycles of deflations and partial restarts. The population is still quite balanced across the four classes, and the number of distinct individuals is also quite stable.

5.3.3.10. *Experiments*

A statistical comparison between the three schemes ("fixed size", "deflating only", and "inflating + deflating") has been performed based on 100 runs. For each run, we share the 16 experiments across a learning set, made up of 10 to 13 randomly-chosen experiments, and a test set, made up of the rest of the experiments. The three strategies are tested on the same sets during 50, 000 evaluations and their parameters are detailed in Table 5.3.

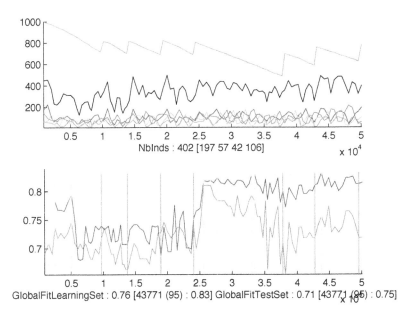

Figure 5.11. *Typical run of a Parisian GP (inflating + deflating scheme). Top: size of the population and number of distinct individuals in each class. Bottom: percentage of correct classifications on the learning set and test set. For a color version of this figure, see www.iste.co.uk/lutton/algorithms.zip*

5.3.3.11. *Results*

Medians, means and standard deviations have been computed for the percentage of correct classifications on the test and learning sets (see Figure 5.12). Number of evaluations and number of generations to reach the best individual, as well as total number of generations for 50, 000 evaluations, are presented in Figure 5.12 and Table 5.4.

Using the fixed-sized population as a reference for comparisons, we observe in Table 5.4 that the deflating + inflating scheme allows us to gain almost 2% on the test set, whereas the deflating-only scheme reaches almost the same score. The same conclusions can be drawn on the learning set. More precisely, in Figure 5.12 it is to be noted again that the classification on the test set is better on average with the deflating + inflating scheme, but also that it has a narrower range of values, i.e it fails less often.

	Fixed size	Deflating-only	Deflating + inflating
Population size	1000	1000, then decreasing	1000, then decreasing and increasing
Clustering parameters	none	$to\_keep = 7$ $to\_remove = 1$	$to\_keep = 7$ $to\_remove = 1$ $to\_insert = 3$
Number of evaluations	50000		
Sharing	$\sigma_{share} = 1$ on the first third of evaluations then linear decrease from 1 to 0.1 $\alpha_{share} = 1$ (constant)		

Table 5.3. *Parameters of the three strategies*

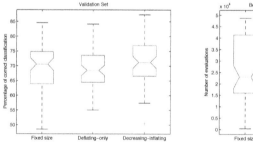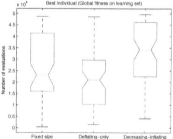

Figure 5.12. *Percentage of correct classification of the best individual in the learning set (left) and number of evaluations needed to reach it (right). Statistics are based on 100 runs. For a color version of this figure, see www.iste.co.uk/lutton/algorithms.zip*

As far as the number of evaluations is concerned, in Table 5.4 and Figure 5.12 decreasing the size of the population and then increasing it enables us to reduce the stagnation effect (the best individual is reached far later). This stagnation effect is clearer with the deflating-only scheme, due to the fact that decreasing the size of the population also decreases its diversity.

	Fixed size			Deflating-only			Deflating+inflating		
	med	mean	SD	med	mean	SD	med	mean	SD
Correct classification (test set)	70.59	68.93	8.48	68.51	68.69	7.32	71.24	70.96	7.95
Correct classification (learning set)	79.49	79.39	2.75	79.17	78.76	3.26	80.33	80.09	3.27
Number of evaluations (best)	23065	25866	14612	21073	20827	12727	34324	33130	13637
Number of generations (best)	39	41.10	22.9	46	68.3	94.8	70	70.1	32.7
Number of generations (total)	74	75.26	7.77	269	356.3	240.7	98	100.9	12.52

Table 5.4. *Experimental results of the three strategies*

5.3.3.12. *Analysis of variance*

A one-way analysis of variance has been used to compare the means of the various test samples[5]. It returns the P-value for the null hypothesis, that is "the two sets are samples with the same mean". We compare strategies two by two, first fixed *versus* deflating-only, then fixed *versus* deflating + inflating, and finally deflating-only *versus* deflating + inflating. Results are given in Table 5.5.

A large P-value (close to 1) corresponds to a high probability of having two samples with the same mean. This is the case for the

---

5 This test supposes that the distributions of the samples are Gaussian, which is obviously not the case here. In the absence of additional hypotheses, the P-value however provides a quite good measurement of the similarities of sample distributions.

classification on the test set for the fixed size and deflating-only schemes. The deflating-only and deflating + inflating have much lower *P*-values, meaning that there is a significant statistical difference.

	Fixed size vs. Deflating-only	Fixed size vs. Deflating-inflating	Deflating-only vs. Deflating-inflating
Correct classification on the test set	0.8602	0.1627	0.0930
Correct classification on the learning set	0.2331	0.1921	0.0219

Table 5.5. *P-values*

5.3.4. *Analysis*

This first attempt to manage varying population sizes within a Parisian GP scheme show the effectiveness of the population deflation + inflation scheme in terms of computational gain and quality of results using a real problem. The deflating scheme allows us to obtain the same result as the fixed-size population strategy, but using fewer fitness evaluations. The deflating + inflating strategy improves the quality of results for the same number of fitness evaluations as the fixed-size strategy.

In general, the development of a single-population cooperative–co-evolution GP scheme is very attractive as it allows us to evolve simpler structures in fewer generations, and yield results that are usually easier to interpret. However, as one "Parisian" generation necessitates more complex operations, one must carefully consider the global gain of such a procedure (in terms of fitness evaluation or even global computation time). The implementation of a population deflating + inflating scheme is another way to spare computational power, as it allows us to avoid redundancy while regularly renewing population diversity.

More generally, the deflation + inflation scheme has two major characteristics: clusterization-based redundancy pruning and selective inflation, which tries to maintain limited-size clusters with low complexity individuals. These two concurrent mechanisms tend to better maintain low-complexity individuals as well as genetic diversity. These characteristics may actually be transposed to classical GP or EAs, particularly to limit GP-bloat effects.

5.4. Bayesian network structure learning using CCEAs

BN structure learning is a NP-hard problem [CHI 04], which has applications in many domains when we try to analyze a large set of samples in terms of statistical dependence or causal relationship. In agrifood industries, for example, the analysis of experimental data using BNs helps to gather together technical expert knowledge and know-how on complex processes [BAU 08].

Evolutionary techniques have been used to solve the BN structure learning problem and were facing crucial problems such as:

– BN representation (an individual being a whole structure as in [LAR 96b], or a substructures, as in [MYE 99]);

– fitness function choice [MYE 99].

Various strategies have been used, based on evolutionary programming [TUC 99], immune algorithms [JIA 05], multiobjective strategies [ROS 07], Lamarkian evolution [WAN 04] or hybrid evolution [WON 04].

We propose using an alternate representation, IMs, in order to solve BN structure learning in two steps. IM learning is still a combinatorial problem, but it is easier to embed within an EA. Furthermore, it is suited to a cooperative co-evolution scheme, which allows us to obtain computationally-efficient algorithms.

5.4.1. *Recalling some probability notions*

The joint distribution of X and Y is the distribution of the intersection of random variables X and Y, i.e. of both random variables X and Y occurring together. The *joint probability* of X and Y is written $P(X, Y)$. The *conditional probability* is the probability of random variable X, given the occurrence of an other random variable Y, and is written $P(X|Y)$.

To say that two random variables are *statistically independent* intuitively means that the occurrence of one random variable makes it neither more nor less probable that the other occurs. If random variables X and Y are independent, then the conditional probability of X given Y is the same as the unconditional probability of X, i.e. $P(X) = P(X|Y)$.

Two random variables X and Y are said to be *conditionally independent* given a third random variable Z if knowing Z gives no more information about X once one knows Y. Specifically, $P(X|Z) = P(X|Y, Z)$. In such a case, we say that X and Y are conditionally independent given Z and write it $X \perp\!\!\!\perp Y \mid Z$.

5.4.2. *Bayesian networks*

A BN is a "graph-based model of a joint multivariate probability distribution that captures properties of conditional independence between variables" [FRI 00]. On the one hand, it is a graphical representation of the joint probability distribution and, on the other hand, it encodes independences between variables. For example, a BN could represent the probabilistic relationships between diseases and symptoms. Given symptoms, the network can be used to compute the probabilities of the presence of various diseases (i.e. inference).

Formally, a BNs is a directed acyclic graph whose nodes represent variables, and whose missing edges encode conditional independence between the variables. This graph, represented in Figure 5.4.2, is called the structure of the network and the nodes containing probabilistic information are called the parameters of the network.

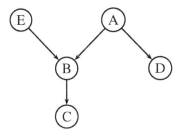

Figure 5.13. *Directed acyclic graph*

The set of parent nodes of node X_i is denoted by $pa(X_i)$. In a BN, the joint probability distribution of the node values can be written as the product of the local probability distribution of each node and its parents:

$$P(X_1, X_2, \ldots, X_n) = \prod_{i=1}^{n} P(X_i|pa(X_i))$$

5.4.2.1. *Uses of BNs*

Using a BN can save considerable amounts of memory, if the dependencies in the joint distribution are sparse. For example, a naive way of storing the conditional probabilities of 10 binary variables as a table requires storage space for $2^{10} = 1024$ values. If the local distributions of no variable depends on more than three parent variables, the BN representation needs to store at most $10 \times 2^3 = 80$ values. One advantage of BNs is that it is intuitively easier for a human to understand (a sparse set of) direct dependencies and local distributions than complete joint distribution.

Lastly, more than just a computing tool, BNs can be used to represent causal relationships and appear to be powerful graphical models of causality.

5.4.2.2. *Parameter and structure learning*

The BN learning problem has two branches: the *parameter* learning problem (i.e., to find the probability tables of each node) and the *structure* learning problem (i.e. to find the graph of the network), following the decomposition of the two constitutive parts of a BN: its structure and its parameters.

There are already algorithms specially suited to the parameter learning problem, like expectation-maximization (EM) that is used to find maximum likelihood estimates of parameters.

Learning the structure is a more challenging problem because the number of possible BN structures (NS) grows superexponentially with the number of nodes [ROB 77]. For example, $NS(5) = 29,281$ and $NS(10) = 4.2 \times 10^{18}$. A direct approach is intractable for more than seven or eight nodes. It is thus necessary to use heuristics in the search space.

In a comparative study by Francois and Leray [FRA 04], the authors identified various structure learning algorithms including *PC* [SPI 01] or *IC/IC** [PEA 91] (causality search using statistical tests to evaluate conditional independence), *BN Power Constructor* [CHE 97] (also uses conditional independence tests) and other methods based on scoring criterion, such as *minimal weight spanning tree* (intelligent weighting of the edges and application of the algorithms for the problem of the minimal weight tree), *K2* [COO 92] (maximization of $P(G|D)$ using Bayes and a topological order on the nodes), *greedy search* [CHI 02] (finding the best neighbor and iterating) or *SEM* [FRI 97] (extension of the EM meta-algorithm to the structure learning problem). However, that may be the problem of learning an optimal BN from a given dataset is NP-hard [CHI 04].

5.4.2.3. *The PC algorithm*

PC, the reference causal discovery algorithm, was introduced by Sprites *et al.* in 1993 [SPI 01]. A similar algorithm, IC, was proposed simultaneously by Pearl and Verma [PEA 91]. It uses Chi-squared tests to evaluate the conditional independence between two nodes. It is then possible to rebuild the structure of the network from the set of conditional independences discovered. The PC algorithm actually starts from a fully connected network and every time a conditional independence is detected, the corresponding edge is removed. The first detailed steps of this algorithm are:

– step 0: start with a complete undirected graph G;

– step 1: test all conditional zero-order independences (i.e $x \perp\!\!\!\perp y \mid \emptyset$, where x and y are two distinct nodes of G). If $x \perp\!\!\!\perp y$, then remove edge $x - y$;

– step 2: test all conditional first-order independences (i.e $x \perp\!\!\!\perp y \mid z$, where x, y, and z are three distinct nodes of G). If $x \perp\!\!\!\perp y \mid z$, then remove edge $x - y$;

– step 3: test all conditional second-order independences (i.e $x \perp\!\!\!\perp y \mid \{z_1, z_2\}$, where x, y, z_1 and z_2 are four distinct nodes of G). If $x \perp\!\!\!\perp y \mid \{z_1, z_2\}$, then remove edge $x - y$;

– ...

– step k: test all conditional K-order independences (i.e $x \perp\!\!\!\perp y \mid \{z_1, z_2, \ldots, z_k\}$, where $x, y, z_1, z_2, \ldots, z_k$, are $k + 2$ distinct nodes of G). If $x \perp\!\!\!\perp y \mid \{z_1, z_2, \ldots, z_k\}$, then remove the edge between $x - y$;

– next steps: take particular care to detect some structures called *V-structures* (see section 5.4.2.4) and recursively detect the orientation of the remaining edges.

The complexity of this algorithm depends on N, the size of the network and k, the upper bound on the fan-in and is equal to $O(N^k)$. In practice, this implies that the value of k must remain very small when dealing with big networks.

5.4.2.4. *Independence models*

As we have seen, a BN represents a factorization of a joint probability distribution, but can many possible factorizations represent the same joint probability distribution. Two structures are said to be *Markov equivalent* if they represent the same joint probability distribution.

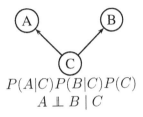

$$P(A|C)P(B|C)P(C)$$
$$A \perp\!\!\!\perp B \mid C$$

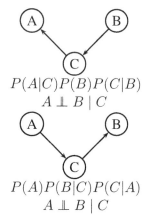

$$P(A|C)P(B)P(C|B)$$
$$A \perp\!\!\!\perp B \mid C$$

$$P(A)P(B|C)P(C|A)$$
$$A \perp\!\!\!\perp B \mid C$$

These tree structures encode the same independence statement (IS) $A \perp\!\!\!\perp B \mid C$.

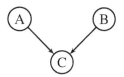

$$P(A)P(B)P(C|A,B)$$
A is NOT independent of B given C

This last structure, called the *V-structure* (or *collider*), is not Markov equivalent to the three prior ones.

Here, we do not work directly on BNs but on a more general model called IM, which can be seen as the underlying model of BNs and is defined as follows:

– let N be a non-empty set of variables. $T(N)$ denotes the collection of all triplets $\langle X, Y|Z \rangle$ of disjoint subsets of N, $X \neq \emptyset$ and $Y \neq \emptyset$. The class of elementary triplets $E(N)$ consists of $\langle x, y|Z \rangle \in T(N)$, where $x, y \in N$ are distinct and $Z \subset N \setminus \{x, y\}$;

– let P be a joint probability distribution over N and $\langle X, Y|Z \rangle \in T(N)$. $\langle X, Y|Z \rangle$ is called an IS if X is conditionally independent of Y given Z with respect to P (i.e $X \perp\!\!\!\perp Y \mid Z$);

– an IM is a subset of $T(N)$: each probability distribution P defines an IM, namely the model $\{\langle X, Y|Z \rangle \in T(N) \; ; \; X \perp\!\!\!\perp Y \mid Z\}$, called the IM induced by P.

In summary, an IM is the set of all the ISs, that is the set of all $\langle X, Y|Z \rangle$ satisfied by P, and different Markov equivalent BNs induce the same IM. By following the paths in a BN, it is possible (even though it can be combinatorial) to find a part of its IM using algorithms based on directional separation (d-separation) or moralization criteria. Reciprocally, IM can be used as a guide to produce the structure of a BN.

Consequently, as the problem of finding an IM can be turned in to an optimization problem, we investigate the use of an EA. More precisely, we build an algorithm that lets a population of triplets $\langle X, Y|Z \rangle$ evolve until the whole population comes near to the IM, which corresponds to a cooperative co-evolution scheme.

5.4.3. *Evolution of an IM*

As in section 5.3, our algorithm (IMPEA) is a Parisian cooperative co-evolution. However, in a pure Parisian scheme (Figure 5.1), a multi-individual evaluation (global fitness computation) is done at each generation and redistributed as a bonus to the individuals who participated in the aggregation. Here, IMPEA only computes the global evaluation at the end of the evolution, and thus does not use any feedback mechanism. This approach, which is an extreme case of the Parisian CCEA, has been successfully used, for example, in real-time EAs, such as the *flies* algorithm [LOU 02].

IMPEA is actually a two-step algorithm. First, it generates a subset of the IM of a BN from data by evolving elementary triplets $\langle x, y|Z \rangle$, where x and y are two distinct nodes and Z is a subset of the other ones, which can be empty. Then, it uses the ISs that it found in the first step to build the structure of a representative network.

5.4.3.1. *Search space and local fitness*

Individuals are elementary triplets $\langle x, y|Z \rangle$. Each individual is evaluated through a Chi-squared test of independence that tests the null hypothesis H_0: "The nodes x and y are independent given Z." The Chi-squared statistic (χ^2) is calculated by finding the difference between each observed O_i and theoretical E_i frequencies for each of the n possible outcomes, squaring them, dividing each by the theoretical frequency, and taking the sum of the results: $\chi^2 = \sum_{i=1}^{n} \frac{(O_i - E_i)^2}{E_i}$. The Chi-squared statistic can then be used to calculate a P-value P by comparing the value of the statistical χ^2 to a Chi-squared distribution with $n - 1$ degrees of freedom, as represented in Figure 5.14.

P represents the probability of making a mistake if the null hypothesis is not accepted. It is then compared to a significance level α (0.05 is often chosen as a cut-off for significance), and independence is rejected if $P < \alpha$. The reader has to keep in mind that rejecting H_0 allows one to conclude that the two variables are dependent, but not rejecting H_0 means that one cannot conclude that these two variables are dependent (which is not exactly the same as claiming that they are independent). Given that the higher the P-value, the stronger the independence, P seems to be a good candidate to represent local fitness (which measures the quality of individuals). Nevertheless, this fitness suffers from two drawbacks:

– when dealing with small datasets, individuals with a long constraining set Z tend to have good P-values only because the dataset is too small to get enough samples to efficiently test the statement $x \perp\!\!\!\perp y \mid Z$;

– due to the exponential behavior of the Chi-squared distribution, its tail vanishes so quickly that individuals with poor P-values are often rounded to 0, making them indistinguishable.

First, P has to be adjusted in order to promote ISs with small Z. This is achieved by setting up a parsimony term as a positive multiplicative malus $parcim(\#Z)$ that decreases with $\#Z$, the number of nodes in Z. Then, when $P < \alpha$, we replace the exponential tail with something that tends to zero slower. This modification of the fitness landscape allows us to avoid plateaux that would prevent the GA traveling all over the search space. Here is the adjusted local fitness[6]:

$$AdjLocalFitness = \begin{cases} p \times parcim(\#Z) & if\ p \geq \alpha \\ \alpha \times parcim(\#Z) \times \frac{X_{\alpha}^2}{X^2} & if\ p < \alpha \end{cases}$$

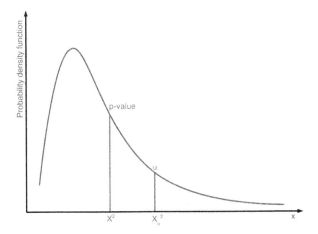

Figure 5.14. *Chi-squared test of independence. For a color version of this figure, see www.iste.co.uk/lutton/algorithms.zip*

5.4.3.2. *Genetic operators*

The genome of an individual, being $\langle x, y | Z \rangle$ where x and y are simple nodes and Z is a set of nodes, is straightforward. It consists of an array of three cells (see Figure 5.15): the first one containing the index of the node x, the second cell containing the index of y and the last one is the array of the indexes of the nodes in Z.

$$\begin{array}{cccc} x & y & Z=\{z_1,z_2,...,z_k\} \\ \boxed{x} & \boxed{y} & \boxed{z_1 \ \vdots \ z_2 \ \vdots \ ... \ \vdots \ z_k} \end{array}$$

Figure 5.15. *Representation of $\langle x, y | Z \rangle$*

---

6 *Note:* This can be viewed as an "Ockham's Razor" argument.

This coding implies specific genetic operators because of the constraints resting upon a chromosome: doubles must not appear with mutations or crossovers. A quick-and-dirty solution is to first apply classical genetic operators and then apply a *repair operator*. Instead, we propose wise operators (which do not create doubles), with two types of mutations and an robust crossover:

– *genome content mutation*: this mutation operator involves a probability p_{mG} that an arbitrary node will be changed from its original state. In order to avoid the creation of doubles, this node can be muted into any nodes in N except the other nodes of the individual, but including itself (see Figure 5.16);

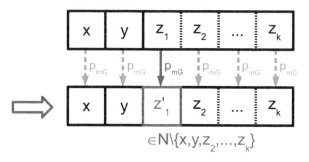

Figure 5.16. *Genome content mutation. For a color version of this figure, see www.iste.co.uk/lutton/algorithms.zip*

– *add/remove mutation*: the previous mutation randomly modifies the content of the individuals, but does not modify the length of the constraining set Z. We introduce a new mutation operator called *add/remove mutation*, represented in Figure 5.17, that allows us to randomly add or remove nodes in Z. If this type of mutation is selected, with probability P_{mAR}, then new random nodes are added with a probability of P_{mAdd} or removed with $1 - P_{mAdd}$. These probabilities can vary along generations. Moreover, the minimal and the maximal number of nodes allowed in Z can also evolve along generations, allowing us to tune the growth of Z;

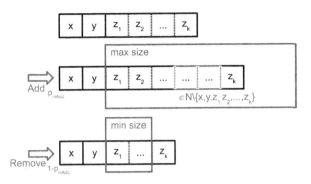

Figure 5.17. *Add/remove mutation. For a color version of this figure, see www.iste.co.uk/lutton/algorithms.zip*

– *crossover*: the crossover consists of a simple swapping mechanism between x, y and Z. Two individuals, $\langle x, y | Z \rangle$ and $\langle x', y' | Z' \rangle$, can exchange x or y with probability p_{cXY} and Z with probability p_{cZ} (see Figure 5.18). When a crossover occurs, only one swap among $x \leftrightarrow x'$, $y \leftrightarrow y'$, $x \leftrightarrow y'$, $y \leftrightarrow x'$ and $Z \leftrightarrow Z'$ is selected via a wheel mechanism implying that $4p_{cXY} + p_{cZ} = 1$. If the exchange is impossible, then the problematic nodes are automatically muted in order to avoid doubles.

5.4.4. *Sharing*

So as not to converge to a single optimum, but enable the GA to identify multiple optima, we use a sharing mechanism that maintains diversity within the population by creating *ecological niches*. The complete scheme is described in [DEB 89] and is based on the fact that fitness is considered a shared resource, i.e. individuals having too many neighbors are penalized. Thus, we need a way to compute the distance between individuals so that we can count the number of neighbors of a given individual. A simple Hamming distance is chosen: two elementary triplets $\langle x, y | Z \rangle$ and $\langle x', y' | Z' \rangle$ are said to be neighbors if they test the same two nodes (i.e. $\{x, y\} = \{x', y'\}$), whatever Z. Finally, dividing the fitness of each individual by the number of its neighbors results in distributing the population into subpopulations whose size is proportional to the height of the peak they are colonizing [GOL 87]. Instead, we take into account the relative importance of an individual with respect to its neighborhood, and the fitness of each individual is divided by the sum of the fitnesses of its neighbors [LUT 96]. This scheme allows us to equilibrate the subpopulations within peaks, whatever their height.

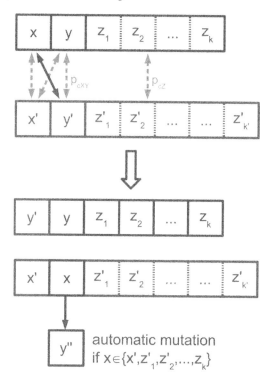

Figure 5.18. *Robust crossover. For a color version of this figure, see www.iste.co.uk/lutton/algorithms.zip*

5.4.5. *Immortal archive and embossing points*

Recall that the aim of IMPEA is to construct a subset of the IM, and thus the more ISs we get, the better it is. Using a classical Parisian EA scheme would allow us to evolve a number of IS equal to the population size. In order to be able to evolve larger IS sets, IMPEA implements an *immortal archive* that gathers the best individuals found so far. An individual $\langle x, y | Z \rangle$ can become immortal if any of the following rules applies:

– its *P*-value is equal to 1 (or numerically greater than $1 - \epsilon$, where ϵ is the precision of the computer);

– its *P*-value is greater than the significance level and $Z = \emptyset$;

– its *P*-value is greater than the significance level and $\langle x, y | \emptyset \rangle$ is already immortal.

This archive serves two purposes: the most obvious one is that at the end of the generations, not only do we get all the individuals of the current population but also all the immortal individuals, which can make a huge difference. But this archive also plays a very important role as *embossing points*: when computing the sharing coefficient, immortal individuals that are not in the current population are added to the neighbor counting. Therefore, a region of the search space that has already been explored but that has disappeared from the current population is *marked as explored* since immortal individuals count as neighbors and thus penalize this region, encouraging the exploration of other zones.

5.4.5.1. *Clustering and partial restart*

Despite the sharing mechanism, we observed experimentally that some individuals became overrepresented within the population. Therefore, we added a mechanism to reduce this undesirable effect: if an individual has too many redundant representatives, then the surplus is eliminated and new random individuals are generated to replace the old ones.

5.4.6. *Description of the main parameters*

Table 5.6 describes the main parameters of IMPEA and their typical values or ranges of values. Some of these parameters are scalars, like the number of individuals, and are constant throughout the evolution process. Other parameters, such as the minimum or maximum number of nodes in Z, are arrays indexed by the number of generations, allowing these parameters to follow a profile of evolution.

Name	Description	Typical value
MaxGens	Number of generations	$50 \ldots 200$
Ninds	Number of individuals	$50 \ldots 500$
Alpha	Significance level of the χ^2 test	$0.01 \ldots 0.25$
Parcim (#Z)	Array of parsimony coefficient (decreases with the length of Z)	$0.5 \ldots 1$
PmG	Probability of genome content mutation	$0.1/(2 + \#Z)$
PmAR	Probability of adding or removing nodes in Z	$0.2 \ldots 0.5$
PmAdd (#Gen)	Array of robability of adding nodes in Z along generations	$0.25 \ldots 0.75$
MinNodes (#Gen)	Array of minimal number of nodes in Z along generations	$0 \ldots 2$
MaxNodes (#Gen)	Array of maximal number of nodes in Z along generations	$0 \ldots 6$
Pc	Probability of crossover	0.7
PcXY	Probability of swapping x and y	$1/6$
PcZ	Probability of swapping Z	$1/3$
Epsilon	Numerical precision	10^{-5}
MaxRedundant	Maximal number of redundant individuals in the population	$1 \ldots 5$

Table 5.6. *Parameters of IMPEA. Values are chosen within their typical range depending on the size of the network and the desired computation time*

5.4.7. *BN structure estimation*

The last step of IMPEA consists of reconstructing the structure of the BN. This is achieved by aggregating all the immortal individuals and only the *good ones* from the final population. An individual, $\langle x, y | Z \rangle$, is said to be *good* if its *P*-value allows us not to reject the null hypothesis $x \perp\!\!\!\perp y \mid Z$. There are two strategies in IMPEA: a pure one, called *P-IMPEA*, which consists of strictly enforcing ISs; and an constrained one, called C-IMPEA, which adds a constraint on the number of desired edges.

5.4.7.1. *Pure conditional independence*

As in PC, P-IMPEA starts from a fully-connected graph, and for each individual of the aggregated population it applies the rule "$x \perp\!\!\!\perp y \mid Z \Rightarrow$ no edge between x and y" to remove edges whose nodes belong to an IS. The remaining edges (which have not been eliminated) constitute the undirected structure of the network.

5.4.7.2. *Estimation of constrained edges*

C-IMPEA needs an additional parameter: the desired number of edges in the final structure. It proceeds by accumulation. It starts from an empty adjacency matrix and for each $\langle x, y \mid Z \rangle$ individual in the aggregated population, it adds its fitness to the entry (x, y). An example of a matrix obtained in this way is shown in Figure 5.19.

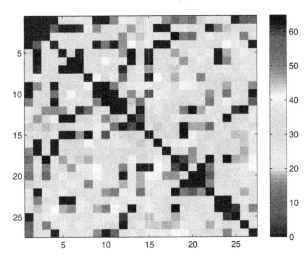

Figure 5.19. *Accumulated adjacency matrix of a network with 27 nodes (from an insurance network). For a color version of this figure, see www.iste.co.uk/lutton/algorithms.zip*

At the end of this process, if an entry (at the intersection of a row and a column) is still equal to zero, then it there was no IS with this pair of nodes in the aggregated population. Thus, these entries correspond to the strict application of the conditional independence. If an entry has a low sum, then it is an entry for which IMPEA found only a few ISs (and/or ISs with low fitness), and thus there is a high expectancy of having an edge between its nodes. To add more edges in the final structure (up to the desired number of edges), we have to select edges with the lowest values and construct the corresponding network.

This approach seems to be more robust, since it allows some "errors" in the Chi-squared tests, but strictly speaking, if an IS is discovered, there cannot be any edge between the two nodes.

5.4.8. *Experiments and results*

5.4.8.1. *Test case: comb network*

To evaluate the efficiency of IMPEA, we forge a test network that looks like a *comb*. A n-comb network has $n + 2$ nodes: x, y, and $z_1, z_2, \ldots, z_n$, as we can see in Figure 5.20. The conditional probability tables (CPTs) are filled in with a uniform law. It can be seen as a kind of classifier: given the input $z_1, z_2, \ldots, z_n$, it classifies the output as x or y. For example, it could be a classifier that accepts a person's salary details, age, marital status, home address and credit history and classifies the person as acceptable/unacceptable to receive a new credit card or loan.

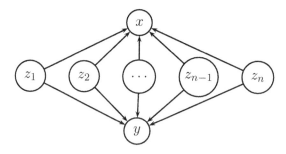

Figure 5.20. *A n-comb network*

Such a network is interesting because its IM can be generated (using semigraphoid rules) from the following ISs:

$$\forall i, j \text{ such as } i \neq j, z_i \perp\!\!\!\perp z_j$$
$$x \perp\!\!\!\perp y \mid \{z_1, z_2, \ldots, z_n\}$$

Thus, it has only one complex IS and a lot of simple (short) ones. The only way to remove the edge between x and y using statistical Chi-squared tests is to test the triplet $\langle x, y \mid \{z_1, z_2, \ldots, z_n\}\rangle$. This cannot be achieved by the PC algorithm when $k < n$ (and in practice, k is limited to 3 due to combinatorial complexity).

Typical run: we choose to test P-IMPEA with a simple 6-comb network. It has been implemented using an open-source toolbox, the Bayes Net Toolbox for Matlab [MUR 01] available at http://bnt.sourceforge.net/. We draw our inspiration from PC and initialize the population with individuals with an empty constraining set and let it grow along generations that have up to six nodes in order to find the IS $x \perp\!\!\!\perp y \mid \{z_1, \ldots, z_6\}$. As shown in Figure 5.21, the minimal number of nodes allowed in Z is always 0, and the maximal number increases during the first two-thirds of the generations and is kept to 6 in the last ones. The average number of nodes in the current population is also slowly rising but remains small since, in this example, there are a lot of small *easy to find* ISs and only a single big one. The correct structure (Figure 5.22) is found after 40 (out of 50) generations.

Figure 5.23 represents the evolution of the number of errors along the generations. The current evolved structure is compared with the actual structure. An *added* edge is an edge present in the evolved structure but not in the actual comb network, and a *deleted* edge is an edge that has been wrongly removed. The total number of errors is the sum of added and deleted edges. Note that even if the number of errors of the discovered edges is extracted at each generation, it is by no means used by IMPEA or reinjected into the population because this information is only relevant in the particular test case where the BN the generated the dataset is known.

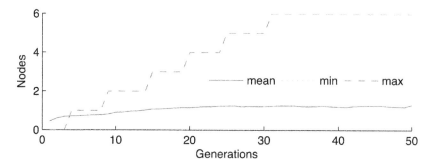

Figure 5.21. *Evolution of minimal, maximal and average number of nodes in Z along generations. For a color version of this figure, see www.iste.co.uk/lutton/algorithms.zip*

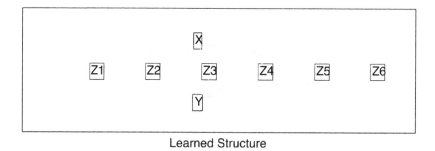

Learned Structure

Figure 5.22. *Final structure for the comb network. For a color version of this figure, see www.iste.co.uk/lutton/algorithms.zip*

Statistical results: the previous example gives an idea of the behavior of P-IMPEA, but to compare it fairly with PC we must compare them not only over multiple runs but also with respect to the size of the dataset. So we set up the following experimental protocol:

– a 4-comb network is created and we use the same BN (structure and CPT) throughout the whole experiment;

– we   chose   representative   sizes   for   the   dataset:
$\{500, 1,000, 2,000, 5,000, 10,000\}$, and for each size, we generate the
corresponding number of cases from the comb network.

– we run both the PC and P-IMPEA 100 times, and extract relevant
information (see Tables 5.7 and 5.8):

- how many edges were found? Among these, how many were
erroneous? (added or deleted),

- did the algorithm remove the edge $x - y$?

– PC is tuned with a fan-in k equal to 3 and P-IMPEA is tuned with
50 generations of 50 individuals in order to take the same computational
time as PC. They both share the same significance level α.

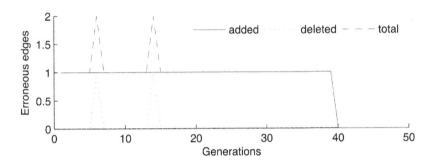

Figure 5.23. *Evolution of the number of erroneous edges of the
structure along the generations. For a color version of this figure, see
www.iste.co.uk/lutton/algorithms.zip*

The actual network contains eight edges and six nodes. Therefore,
the number of possible alternative is $2^6 = 64$, and if we roughly want
to have 30 samples per possibility we would need approximatively
$64 * 30 \approx 2,000$ samples. That explains why performances of the
Chi-squared test are very poor with only 500 and 1,000 cases in the
dataset. When the dataset is too small, PC removes the $x - y$ edge (see
the last row of Table 5.7) while it does not even test
$\langle x, y \mid \{z_1, z_2, z_3, z_4\}\rangle$ because it is limited by k to 3 nodes in Z.

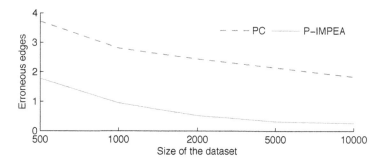

Figure 5.24. *The number of wrong edges (added and deleted) for PC and P-IMPEA, depending on the size of the dataset. For a color version of this figure, see www.iste.co.uk/lutton/algorithms.zip*

Figure 5.24 shows the average number of wrong nodes (either *added* or *deleted*) of both algorithms. As expected, the number of errors decreases with the size of the dataset, and it is clear that P-IMPEA outperforms PC in every case.

Cases	Edges	Added	Removed	Errors	x–y?
500	5.04 ± 0.85	0.38 ± 0.50	3.34 ± 0.78	3.72 ± 1.01	97%
1000	6.50 ± 1.24	0.66 ± 0.71	2.16 ± 1.01	2.82 ± 1.23	83%
2000	8.09 ± 1.18	1.27 ± 0.80	1.18 ± 0.68	2.45 ± 0.91	39%
5000	9.71 ± 0.74	1.93 ± 0.57	0.22 ± 0.46	2.15 ± 0.73	0%
10000	9.84 ± 0.58	1.84 ± 0.58	0 ± 0	1.84 ± 0.58	0%

Table 5.7. *Averaged results of PC algorithm after 100 runs*

Cases	Edges	Added	Removed	Errors	x–y?
500	6.64 ± 0.79	0.05 ± 0.21	1.73 ± 1.90	1.78 ± 1.94	100%
1000	7.32 ± 0.91	0.18 ± 0.50	0.78 ± 1.01	0.96 ± 1.24	100%
2000	8.87 ± 1.04	0.24 ± 0.51	0.29 ± 0.60	0.53 ± 0.82	97%
5000	8.29 ± 0.32	0.30 ± 0.59	0.03 ± 0.17	0.33 ± 0.63	90%
10000	8.27 ± 0.31	0.27 ± 0.54	0 ± 0	0.27 ± 0.54	89%

Table 5.8. *Averaged results of P-IMPEA algorithm after 100 runs*

Finally, the average number of discovered edges is almost equal to eight (which is the actual number of edges in the 4-comb structure) for P-IMPEA, whereas it is greater than nine for the PC algorithm since it cannot remove the $x - y$ edge.

5.4.8.2. *Classical benchmark: the insurance BN*

Insurance [BIN 97] is a network for evaluating car insurance risks. The insurance BN contains 27 variables and 52 arcs (Figure 5.25). In our experiments we use a database containing 50,000 cases generated from the network.

Once again, we start from a population with small Z and let it increase up to four nodes. Figure 5.26 illustrates this growth: the average size of the number of nodes in Z of the current population follows the orders given by the minimum and the maximum values.

The evolution of the number of wrong edges, represented in Figure 5.27, quickly decreases during the first half of the generation (the completely connected graph has more than 700 edges) and then stagnates. At the end, P-IMPEA finds 39 edges out of 52, among which there are no added edges, but 13 have wrongly been removed. It is slightly better than PC, which also wrongly removes 13 edges, but which adds one superfluous one.

The best results are obtained with C-IMPEA and a desired number of edges equal to 47. Then, only nine errors are made (see Table 5.9). When asking for 52 edges, the actual number of edges in the insurance network, it makes 14 errors (seven additions and seven deletions).

Algorithm	Edges	Added	Removed	Errors
PC	40	1	13	14
P-IMPEA	39	0	13	13
C-IMPEA	47	2	7	9
C-IMPEA	52	7	7	14

Table 5.9. *Number of edges detected for all algorithms*

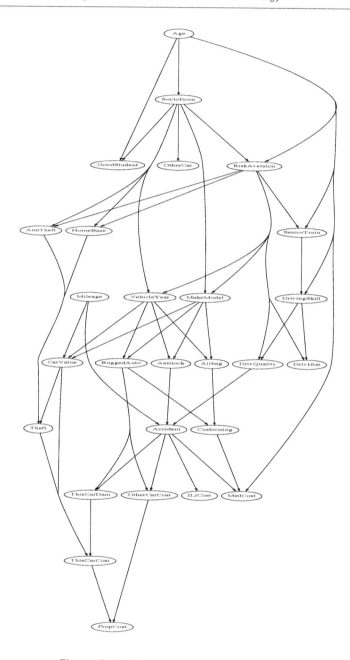

Figure 5.25. *The insurance Bayesian network*

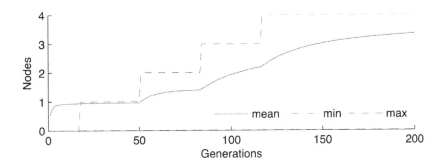

Figure 5.26. *Evolution of minimal, maximal and average number of nodes in Z along the generations. For a color version of this figure, see www.iste.co.uk/lutton/algorithms.zip*

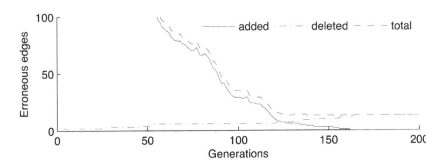

Figure 5.27. *Evolution of the number of wrong edges in the structure along the generations. For a color version of this figure, see www.iste.co.uk/lutton/algorithms.zip*

5.4.8.3. *Real dataset: cheese ripening data from the INCALIN project*

The last step is to test our algorithm on real data. Our aim is to compare the result of IMPEA with a part of the dynamic BN described in section 5.3, built with human expertise within the scope of the INCALIN project. We are interested in the part of the network that predicts the current phase, knowing the derivatives of some bacteria proportions. We used the same data as in the first part of the report (see section 5.3.2.5), made up of the derivatives of pH, la, *K. marxianus* and *B. auriantiacum* and the estimation of the current phase done by an expert.

After 10 generations of 25 individuals each, P-IMPEA converges to a network whose structure is almost the same as the one proposed by the experts. As we can see on the right in Figure 5.28, no extra edge is added, but it misses the edge between the derivative of *la* and the phase.

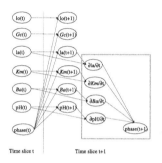
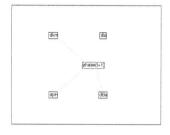

(a) Dynamic Bayesian Network proposed by cheese ripening experts.

(b) Results of P-IMPEA.

Figure 5.28. *Comparison between the model proposed by the experts and the network found by IMPEA on a real dataset from the INCALIN project*

5.4.9. *Analysis*

We compared performances on the basis of undirected graphs produced by both algorithms. The edge directions estimation has not been yet programmed in IMPEA. This will be done in future developments, using a low combinatorial strategy similar to PC. Comparisons between both algorithms do not actually depend on this step.

The two experiments in section 5.4.8 prove that IMPEA compares favorably to PC, despite the fact that IMPEA relies on a convenient problem encoding, PC performs a deterministic and systematic search while IMPEA uses evolutionary mechanisms to prune computational efforts and to concentrate on promising parts of the search space. The limitation of PC according to problem size is obvious in the first test (comb network): PC is unable to capture a complex dependency, even on a small network. Additionally, it is to be noted that IMPEA better resists a current problem of real-life data: the insufficient number of samples available.

5.5. Conclusion

Parisian CCEAs and cooperative–co-evolution in general, when applicable, yield efficient and robust algorithms. As we have seen in this chapter, the main concern is the design of adequate representations for cooperative–co-evolution schemes, i.e. representations that allow a collective evolution mechanism. An evolution mechanism has to be designed that uses pieces of solutions instead of complete solutions as an individual. It also needs to evaluate the pieces of solutions (local fitness) before being able to select the best pieces that can be considered as components of a global solution. To draw a parallel with classical EA approaches, the global fitness is usually equivalent to the fitness of the conventional approach, and partial evaluations (local fitness) allow us to take into account additional prior information about the problem to be solved.

In section 5.3, we first designed a classical GP where the phase estimator was searched as a single best "monolithic" function. Although it already outperforms the previous methods, we made additional improvements by splitting the phase estimation into four combined (and simpler) "phase detectors". We use additional prior information about the problem: The structures searched were binary output functions (or binarized functions) that characterize one of the four phases, and the aggregation is made via a voting scheme, which is more robust. The resulting phase detector has almost the same recognition rate as the classical GP but with a lower variance, evolves simpler structure over fewer generations, and yields results that are easier to interpret.

As we noted some stagnation phenomena due to overspecialization of the best individuals, we were able to design a variable-sized population strategy, using adaptive deflating and inflating schemes for population size. The idea was to group individuals with the same characteristics into "clusters" and remove the most useless ones at the end of every generation while periodically adding "fresh blood" to the population (i.e. new random individuals) if a stagnation criterion was fulfilled.

In section 5.4, IMPEA has allowed us to overcome some drawbacks of the classical approach (i.e. to find an efficient representation of a direct acyclic graph). We have shown that the cooperative scheme is adapted to an alternate representation of BNs: IMs. IMs represent data dependencies via a set of ISs and ISs are naturally suited to be individuals of a CCEA.

The major difficulty in building a BN representative at each generation has been overcome by a scheme that only builds a global solution at the end of the evolution (second step of IMPEA). Future work on this topic will be focused on improving global fitness management within IMPEA. The major improvement of IMPEA is actually that it only performs difficult combinatorial computations when local mechanisms have pushed the population toward an "interesting" area of the search space, thus avoiding complex global computations being made on "bad" solutions. In this sense, CCEAs take into account prior information avoiding computational waste, i.e. complex computations in unfavorable areas of the search space.

Conclusion

There is no doubt that in the domain of food science evolutionary algorithms (EAs) have proven efficient as an optimization tool for single- or multiobjective problems. Our aim with this book is twofold: first, we hope to direct attention to less classical features of EAs, such as cooperative evolution schemes, that allow an optimization problem to be turned into an evolutionary problem in a different, often more computationally efficient way. Human expertise and man–machine interactions are the second topic we aim to showcase in this book. The quantities to be optimized are very difficult to turn into equations, as they are often variable, user-dependent and consider perceptive (taste, flavor), social (sustainability) or expert assessments. We are convinced that interactive evolutionary schemes are a rich ground for developing interactive modeling and decision making.

Let us wrap up this work with a translation of a short story used by Roland Gori to introduce one of his talks. Roland Gori is a psychoanalyst, emeritus professor of psychology at Aix-Marseille university, and specialist in social and psychological issues related to evaluation.

This is the story of two citizens, both named Francis, who live in the same village: one of them is a taxi driver, the other a priest. They die on the same day, and appear before the Lord. Francis the taxi driver comes first. The Lord consults the register and says, "You have deserved Heaven. Here is your argent garment and your platinum stick" Then comes Francis the priest. The Lord consults the register and says, "You have deserved Paradise. Here is your linen garment and your oak stick." Francis the priest is surprised and says: "Lord, there may be a mistake. I know Francis very well. He was an alcoholic, he had several car accidents, led a debauched life, was violent and an unbeliever. He terrorized everybody, while I was spreading Your faith, served Your cause, celebrated Your Mass. I was faithful, chaste. I got a linen garment and an oak stick while he got silver and platinum?" The lord consults the register again and says. "My son, there is no mistake, we changed the evaluation method. We now use a quantitative performance indicator. Each time you celebrated the Mass on Sunday, everybody was falling asleep, while each time he drove, everyone was praying!"

Optimization algorithms are tools, and only tools; even if they were able to give a "perfect" answer (which is not the case for heuristics), they could be the source of wrong decisions. The anthropological concept of "value" cannot be reduced to measurements and numbers, as there is a huge difference between formal objectivity and numerical objectivity. This is particularly evident in the food domain. Evaluating processes, models, food quality and impacts with numbers only is utopistic. Optimization should not be used to impoverish our capacity to make decisions, but to enlarge it. This is our ultimate responsibility, as developers of optimization algorithms.

Bibliography

[ABB 12] ABBASI H., ARDABILI S.M.S.E.-D.-Z.E.A., "Prediction of extensograph properties of wheat-flour dough: artificial neural networks and a genetic algorithm approach", *Journal of Texture Studies*, vol. 43, no. 4, pp. 326–337, 2012.

[ABE 11] ABELHAUSER A., GORI R., SAURET M.-J., *La Folie Évaluation: Les Nouvelles Fabriques De La Servitude. Essai*, Mille et une nuits, http://www.appeldesappels.org/publications/la-folie-evaluation-les-nouvelles-fabriques-de-la-servitude–1262.htm, 2011.

[AGH 11] AGHBASHLO M., MOBLI H.M.A.E.A., "Integrated optimization of fish oil microencapsulation process by spray drying", *Journal of Microencapsulation*, vol. 29, no. 8, pp. 790–804, 2011.

[ALD 06] ALDARF M., FOURCADE F., AMRANE A. *et al.*, "Substrate and metabolite diffusion within model medium for soft cheese in relation to growth of Penicillium camembertii", *J. Ind. Microbiol. Biotechnol.*, vol. 33, pp. 685–692, 2006.

[ALG 15] ALGHOONEH A., BEHBAHANI B.A.N.H., "Application of intelligent modeling to predict the population dynamics of Pseudomonas aeruginosa in Frankfurter sausage containing Satureja bachtiarica extracts", *Microbial Pathogenesis*, vol. 85, pp. 58–65, 2015.

[ALT 95] ALTENBERG L., "The schema theorem and price's theorem", WHITLEY D., VOSE M. (eds), Morgan Kaufmann, *Foundation of Genetic Algorithms 3*, San Francisco, pp. 23–49, 1995.

[ALT 00] ALTENBERG L., "Evolutionary computation models from population genetics. part 2: an historical toolbox", in *Congress on Evolutionary Computation*, Tutorial, 2000.

[AND 06] ANDRÉ C., *Imparfaits, Libres et Heureux: Pratiques De L'estime De Soi*, Odile Jacob, 2006.

[ANG 96] ANGELINE P.J., "Evolving fractal movies", in KOZA J.R., GOLDBERG D.E., FOGEL D.B. *et al*, (eds), *Genetic Programming 1996: Proceedings of the First Annual Conference*, pp. 503–511, 1996.

[ARF 03] ARFI K., AMRITA F., SPINNLER H., "Catabolism of volatile sulfur compounds precursors by Brevibacterium linens and Geotrichum candidum, two microorganisms of the cheese ecosystem.", *J. Biotechnol.*, vol. 105, no. 3, pp. 245–253, 2003.

[BAE 91] BAECK T., HOFFMEISTER F., SCHWEFEL H.P., "A survey of evolution strategies", in *International Conference on Genetic Algorithms*, pp. 2–10, 13–16 July 1991.

[BAG 67] BAGLEY J.D., The behaviour of adaptative systems which employ genetic and correlation algorithms, PhD thesis, University of Michigan, 5106B, 1967.

[BAN 97] BANZHAF W., "Interactive evolution", in *Handbook of Evolutionary Computation*, Oxford University Press, 1997.

[BAR 06] BARILE D., COISSON J., ARLORIO M., RINALDI M., "Identification of production area of Ossolano Italian cheese with chemometric complex approach", *Food Control*, vol. 17, no. 3, pp. 197–206, 2006.

[BAR 09] BARRIERE O., LUTTON E., WUILLEMIN P.-H., "Bayesian network structure learning using cooperative coevolution", *Genetic and Evolutionary Computation Conference (GECCO)*, 2009.

[BAU 08] BAUDRIT C., WUILLEMIN P.-H., SICARD M., PERROT N., *A Dynamic Bayesian Network to Represent a Ripening Process of a Soft Mould Cheese*, Springer, Berlin, Heidelberg, pp. 265–272, 2008.

[BAU 10] BAUDRIT C., SICARD M., WUILLEMIN P. *et al*, "Towards a global modeling of the Camembert-type cheese ripening process by coupling heterogeneous knowledge with dynamic Bayesian networks", *J. Food Eng.*, vol. 98, no. 3, pp. 283–293, 2010.

[BEL 09] BELLOTTI F., BERTA R., DE GLORIA A. *et al.*, "Adaptive experience engine for serious games", *Computational Intelligence and AI in Games, IEEE Transactions on*, vol. 1, no. 4, pp. 264–280, 2009.

[BEY 00] BEYER H.-G., "Evolutionary algorithms in noisy environments: theoretical issues and guidelines for practice", *Computer Methods in Applied Mechanics and Engineering*, vol. 186, nos. 2–4, pp. 239–267, 2000.

[BEY 01] BEYER H.-G., "On the performance of $(1, \lambda)$-evolution strategies for the ridge function class", *IEEE Transactions on Evolutionary Computation*, vol. 5, no. 3, pp. 218–235, 2001.

[BEZ 10] BEZERIANOS A., CHEVALIER F., DRAGICEVIC P. *et al.*, "GraphDice: a system for exploring multivariate social networks", *Computer Graphics Forum (Proc. EuroVis 2010)*, vol. 29, no. 3, pp. 863–872, 2010.

[BIN 97] BINDER J., KOLLER D., RUSSELL S. *et al.*, "Adaptive probabilistic networks with hidden variables", *Machine Learning*, vol. 29, pp. 213–244, 1997.

[BON 05] BONGARD J., LIPSON H., "Active coevolutionary learning of deterministic finite automata", *J. Mach. Learn. Res.*, vol. 6, pp. 1651–1678, 2005.

[BOU 01] BOUMAZA A.M., LOUCHET J., "Dynamic flies: using real-time parisian evolution in robotics", in BOERS E.J., CAGNONI S., GOTTLIEB J. *et al.* (eds), *Applications of Evolutionary Computing. EvoWorkshops 2001: EvoCOP, EvoFlight, EvoIASP, EvoLearn, and EvoSTIM. Proceedings*, vol. 2037, pp. 288–297, 18–19 April 2001.

[BOU 05] BOUTROU R., GUÉGUEN M., "Interests in Geotrichum candidum for cheese technology", *International Journal of Food Microbiology*, vol. 102, no. 1, pp. 1–20, 2005.

[BRE 92] BRETON P., *L'Utopie de la communication*, La Découverte/poche, Paris, 1992.

[BUC 05] BUCCI A., POLLACK J.B., "On identifying global optima in cooperative coevolution", in *Proceedings of the 7th Annual Conference on Genetic and Evolutionary Computation*, GECCO '05, New York, USA, ACM, pp. 539–544, 2005.

[BUT 87] BUTCHER J.C., *The Numerical analysis of Ordinary Differential Equations: Runge-Kutta and General Linear Methods*, Wiley-Interscience, New York, 1987.

[CAN 12] CANCINO W., BOUKHELIFA N., LUTTON E., "EvoGraphDice: interactive evolution for visual analytics", *IEEE Congress on Evolutionary Computation*, 10–15 June 2012.

[CAV 70] CAVICCIO D.J., Adaptative search using simulated evolution, PhD thesis, University of Michigan, 1970.

[CER 95] CERF R., "Asymptotic convergence of genetic algorithms", in *Artificial evolution, European conference, AE 95, Brest, France, September 1995, selected papers Lecture Notes in Computer Science*, Springer Verlag, vol. 1063, pp. 37–54, 1995.

[CHE 97] CHENG J., BELL D.A., LIU W., "An algorithm for Bayesian belief network construction from data", *Proceedings of AI & STAT'97*, pp. 83–90, 1997.

[CHE 10] CHEN D., HUANG G., CHEN Q. *et al.*, "implementing eco-friendly reservoir operation by using genetic algorithm with dynamic mutation operator", in LI K., JIA L., SUN X. *et al.* (eds), *Life System Modeling and Intelligent Computing*, vol. 6330, Springer, Berlin/Heidelberg, pp. 509–516, 2010.

[CHI 94] CHICKERING D.M., GEIGER D., HECKERMAN D., Learning Bayesian Networks is NP-Hard, Report no. MSR-TR-94-17, Microsoft Research, November 1994.

[CHI 02] CHICKERING D.M., "Learning equivalence classes of Bayesian-network structures", *J. Mach. Learn. Res.*, vol. 2, pp. 445–498, March 2002.

[CHI 04] CHICKERING D.M., HECKERMAN D., MEEK C., "Large-sample learning of bayesian networks is NP-hard", *J. Mach. Learn. Res.*, vol. 5, pp. 1287–1330, 2004.

[CHI 05] CHIANG C.-H., SHAUGHNESSY P., LIVINGSTON G. *et al.*, Visualizing Graphical Probabilistic Models., Report no. Technical Report 2005-017, UML CS, 2005.

[CHI 12] CHIMANI M., GUTWENGER C., JÜNGER M. *et al.*, *The Open Graph Drawing Framework (OGDF)*, CRC Press, 2012.

[CHO 97a] CHOISY C., DESMAZEAUD M., GRIPON J. *et al.*, "La biochimie de l'affinage", in Eck A., Gillis J.C. (eds), *Le fromage*, Lavoisier, Paris, pp. 86–105, 1997.

[CHO 97b] CHOISY C., DESMAZEAUD M., GUEGUEN M. *et al.*, "Les phénomènes microbiens", in ECK A., GILLIS J.C. (eds), Le fromage, Lavoisier, Paris, pp. 377–446, 1997.

[COH 87] COHOON J.P., HEGDE S.U., MARTIN W.N. *et al.*, " Punctuated equilibra: a parallel genetic algorithm ", in *Proc. of the 2nd International Conference on Genetic Algorithms and their Applications*, Cambridge, MA, pp. 148–154, 1987.

[COL 00] COLLET P., LUTTON E., RAYNAL F. *et al.*, "Polar IFS + parisian genetic programming = efficient IFS inverse problem solving", *Genetic Programming and Evolvable Machines Journal*, vol. 1, no. 4, pp. 339–361, 2000.

[COO 92] COOPER G.F., HERSKOVITS E., "A Bayesian method for the induction of probabilistic networks from data", *Machine Learning*, vol. 9, pp. 309–347, 1992.

[COO 98] COOPER C.L., *Theories of Organizational Stress*, OUP, Oxford, 1998.

[COS 11] COSSALTER M., MENGSHOEL O.J., SELKER T., "Visualizing and understanding large-scale Bayesian networks", in *The AAAI-11 Workshop on Scalable Integration of Analytics and Visualization*, pp. 12–21, 2011.

[DAR 59] DARWIN C., *The Origin of Species*, available at: literature.org/authors/darwin-charles/the-origin-of-species, 1959.

[DAT 07] DATTA D., DEB K., FONSECA C.M. *et al.*, "Multi-objective evolutionary algorithm for land-use management problem", *International Journal of Computational Intelligence Research*, vol. 3, no. 4, 2007.

[DAV 87] DAVIS L., *Genetic Algorithms and Simulated Annealing*, Morgan Kaufmann, Los Altos, 1987.

[DAV 89] DAVIS L., "Adapting operator probabilities in genetic algorithms", in *Proceedings of the Third International Conference on Genetic Algorithms*, Morgan Kaufmann, San Francisco, pp. 61–69, 1989.

[DAV 91] DAVIS T.E., PRINCIPE J.C., "A simulated annealing like convergence theory for the simple genetic algorithm", in *Proceedings of the Fourth International Conference on Genetic Algorithm*, pp. 174–182, 13–16 July 1991.

[DEB 89] DEB K., GOLDBERG D.E., "An investigation of niche and species formation in genetic function optimization", in *Proceedings of the 3rd International Conference on Genetic Algorithms*, Morgan Kaufmann, San Francisco, pp. 42–50, 1989.

[DEB 00] DEB K., AGRAWAL S., PRATAP A. *et al.*, "A fast Elitist non-dominated sorting genetic algorithm for multi-objective optimization: NSGA-II", in SCHOENAUER M., DEB K., RUDOLF G. *et al.* (eds), *Parallel Problem Solving from Nature – PPSN VI 6th International Conference*, LNCS 1917, Paris, France, Springer Verlag, 16–20 September 2000.

[DEB 01] DEB K., "Multi-objective optimization", in *Multi-objective Optimization Using Evolutionary Algorithms*, John Wiley & Sons, Hoboken, pp. 13–46, 2001.

[DEB 02] DEB K., PRATAP A., AGARWAL S. *et al.*, "A fast and elitist multiobjective genetic algorithm: NSGA-II", *Evolutionary Computation, Transactions on IEEE*, vol. 6, no. 2, pp. 182–197, 2002.

[DEJ 07] DE JONG E.D., STANLEY K.O., WIEGAND R.P., "Introductory tutorial on coevolution", *Proceedings of the 2007 GECCO Conference Companion on Genetic and Evolutionary Computation*, London, UK, 2007.

[DEL 07] DELAPLACE A., BROUARD T., CARDOT H., "Evolutionary methods for learning Bayesian network structures", *Computational Intelligence and Security*, Springer-Verlag, Berlin, Heidelberg, pp. 288–297, 2007.

[DES 37] DESCARTES R., *Le discours de la méthode*, http://classiques.uqac.ca/classiques/Descartes/discours_methode/Discours_methode.pdf, 1637.

[DIC 99] DICKINSON E., "Caseins in emulsions: interfacial properties and interactions", *International Dairy Journal*, vol. 9, nos. 3–6, pp. 305–312, 1999.

[DIC 01] DICKINSON E., "Milk protein interfacial layers and the relationship to emulsion stability and rheology", *Colloids and Surfaces B – Biointerfaces*, vol. 20, no. 3, pp. 197–210, 2001.

[DIC 11] DICKINSON E., "Mixed biopolymers at interfaces: Competitive adsorption and multilayer structures", *Food Hydrocolloids*, vol. 25, no. 8, pp. 1966–1983, 2011.

[DRE 79] DREYFUS H., *What Computers Can't Do*, MIT Press, New York, https://en.wikipedia.org/wiki/Hubert_Dreyfus%27s_views_on_artificial_intelligence, 1979.

[DRU 99] DRUZDZEL M.J., "SMILE: structural modeling, inference, and learning engine and GeNIe: A development environment for graphical decision-theoretic models.", *Proc. of AAAI'99*, pp. 902–903, 1999.

[DUN 06] DUNN E., OLAGUE G., LUTTON E., "Parisian camera placement for vision metrology", *Pattern Recognition Letters*, vol. 27, no. 11, pp. 1209–1219, 2006.

[EIB 04] EIBEN A.E., MARCHIORI E., VALKÓ V.A., *Evolutionary Algorithms with On-the-fly Population Size Adjustment*, pp. 41–50, Springer Berlin, Heidelberg, 2004.

[ELL 77] ELLUL J., *Le Système technicien*, Calmann-Lévy, 1977.

[ELL 04] ELLIS D., BROADHURST D., GOODACRE R., "Rapid and quantitative detection of the microbial spoilage of beef by Fourier transform infrared spectroscopy and machine learning", *Analytica Chimica Acta*, vol. 514, no. 2, pp. 193–201, 2004.

[ELM 08] ELMQVIST N., DRAGICEVIC P., FEKETE J.-D., "Rolling the dice: multidimensional visual exploration using scatterplot matrix navigation", *IEEE Transactions on Visualization and Computer Graphics (Proc. InfoVis 2008)*, vol. 14, no. 6, pp. 1141–1148, 2008.

[ERI 97] ERIKSSON R., OLSSON B., "Cooperative coevolution in inventory control optimisation", in *Proceedings of the Third International Conference on Artificial Neural Networks and Genetic Algorithms*, pp. 583–587, 1997.

[ERN 11] ERNI P., WINDHAB E.J., FISCHER P., "Emulsion drops with complex interfaces: globular versus flexible proteins", *Macromolecular Materials and Engineering*, vol. 296, nos. 3–4, pp. 249–262, 2011.

[ESH 93] ESHELMAN L.J., SCHAFFER J.D., "Real-coded genetic algorithms and interval-schemata", in *Foundations of Genetic Algortihms 2*, Morgan Kaufmann, San Francisco, pp. 187–202, 1993.

[ESP 12] ESPINAR J., COTTA C., FERNÁNDEZ-LEIVA A., "User-centric optimization with evolutionary and memetic systems", *Large-Scale Scientific Computing*, Springer, pp. 214–221, 2012.

[FAN 07] FAN X.F., ET AL., "A direct first principles study on the structure and electronic properties of $Be_xZn_{1--x}O$", *Applied Physics Letters*, vol. 91, no. 12, 2007.

[FEN 13] FENG YAO-ZE, SUN D.-W., "Near-infrared hyperspectral imaging in tandem with partial least squares regression and genetic algorithm for non-destructive determination and visualization of Pseudomonas locontaminationsads in chicken fillets", *Talanta*, vol. 109, pp. 74–83, 2013.

[FOU 11] FOUCQUIER J., GAUCEL S., SUREL C. *et al.*, "Modeling the formation of fat droplet interface during homogenisation in order to describe the texture", in SARAVACOS, G., TAOUKIS P., KROKIDA M. *et al.* (eds), *11th International Congress on Engineering and Food (ICEF11)*, vol. 1 of *Procedia Food Science*, Amsterdam, Netherlands, Elsevier, pp. 706–712, 2011.

[FOU 12] FOUCQUIER J., CHANTOISEAU E., FEUNTEUN S.L. *et al.*, "Toward an integrated modeling of the dairy product transformations, a review of the existing mathematical models", *Food Hydrocolloids*, vol. 27, no. 1, pp. 1–13, 2012.

[FR 06] *Applications of Evolutionary Computing*, vol. 3907, Springer Verlag, Budapest, 10–12 April 2006.

[FRA 04] FRANCOIS O., LERAY P., Etude comparative d'algorithmes d'apprentissage de structure dans les réseaux Bayésiens, Laboratoire Perception, CNRS 2645, 2004.

[FRI 97] FRIEDMAN N., "Learning belief networks in the presence of missing values and hidden variables", in *Proceedings of the Fourteenth International Conference on Machine Learning*, ICML, San Francisco, Morgan Kaufmann, pp. 125–133, 1997.

[FRI 00] FRIEDMAN N., LINIAL M., NACHMAN I., PE'ER D., "Using Bayesian networks to analyze expression data", *Journal of Computational Biology*, vol. 7, nos. 3–4, pp. 601–620, 2000.

[FRU 91] FRUCHTERMAN T.M.J., REINGOLD E.M., "Graph drawing by force-directed placement", *Softw. Pract. Exper.*, vol. 21, no. 11, pp. 1129–1164, 1991.

[GÜR 00] GÜRSOY A., ATUN M., "Neighbourhood preserving load balancing: a self-organizing approach", in *Proceedings from the 6th International Euro-Par Conference on Parallel Processing*, Euro-Par '00, London, Springer-Verlag, pp. 234–241, 2000.

[GAU 14] GAUCEL S., KEIJZER M., LUTTON E. *et al.*, "Learning dynamical systems using standard symbolic regression", in *EuroGP track of EvoStar, The Leading European Event on Bio-Inspired Computation*, LNCS, Springer, Granada, Spain, 23–25 April 2014.

[GAY 09] GAYGADZHIEV Z., HILL A., CORREDIG M., "Influence of the emulsion droplet type on the rheological characteristics and microstructure of rennet gels from reconstituted milk", *Journal of Dairy Research*, vol. 76, no. 3, pp. 349–355, 2009.

[GHA 14] GHASEMI-VARNAMKHASTI M., FORINA M., "NIR spectroscopy coupled with multivariate computational tools for qualitative characterization of the aging of beer", *Computers and Electronics in Agriculture*, vol. 100, pp. 34–40, 2014.

[GOL 87] GOLDBERG D.E., RICHARDSON J., "Genetic algorithms with sharing for multimodal function optimization", in GREFENSTETTE J.J., *Proceedings of the Second International Conference on Genetic Algorithms on Genetic Algorithms and Their Application*, Hillsdale, L. Erlbaum Associates Inc., pp. 41–49, 1987.

[GOL 89] GOLDBERG D.A., *Genetic Algorithms in Search, Optimization, and Machine Learning*, Addison-Wesley, Reading, 1989.

[GRE 85] GREFENSTETTE J.J., FITZPATRICK J.M., "Genetic search with approximate function evaluations", *Proceedings of an International Conference on Genetic Algorithms and Their Applications*, pp. 112–120, 1985.

[GRI 93] GRIPON J.C., "Mould-Ripened Cheeses", in FOX P.F. (ed.), *Cheese: Chemistry, Physics and Microbiology*, Springer, Boston, pp. 111–136, 1993.

[GRI 99] GRIFFITHS A., GELBART W., MILLER J., *et al.*, *Modern Genetic Analysis*, W. H. Freeman, New York, available at http://www.ncbi.nlm.nih.gov/books/NBK21248/, 1999.

[HAN 03] HANSEN N., MÜLLER S.D., KOUMOUTSAKOS P., "Reducing the time complexity of the derandomized evolution strategy with covariance matrix adaptation (CMA-ES)", *Evolutionary Computation*, vol. 11, no. 1, pp. 1–18, 2003.

[HAR 05] HART W., KRASNOGOR N., SMITH J., "Memetic evolutionary algorithms", in *Recent Advances in Memetic Algorithms, Studies in Fuzziness and Soft Computing*, Springer, Berlin, Heidelberg, vol. 166, pp. 3–27, 2005.

[HAY 00] HAYASHIDA N., TAKAGI H., "Visualized IEC: interactive evolutionary computation with multidimensional data visualization", *IECON, 26th Annual Conference of the IEEE*, vol. 4, pp. 2738–2743, 2000.

[HOF 91] HOFFMEISTER F., BÄCK T., "Genetic algorithms and evolution strategies: similarities and differences", SCHWEFEL H.P., MÄNNER R. (eds), *Parallel Problem Solving from Nature – Proceedings of 1st Workshop, PPSN 1, Lecture Notes in Computer Science*, Dortmund, Springer-Verlag, Berlin, vol. 496, pp. 455–469, 1–3 October 1991.

[HOL 62] HOLLAND J.H., "Outline for a logical theory of adaptive systems", *Journal of the Association for the Computing Machinery*, vol. 9, no. 3, pp. 297–314, 1962.

[HOL 75] HOLLAND J.H., *Adaptation in Natural and Artificial System*, University of Michigan Press, Ann Arbor, 1975.

[HOL 77] HOLLAND J.H., REITMAN J.S., "Cognitive systems based on adaptive algorithms", *SIGART Bull.*, no. 63, pp. 49–49, 1977.

[HON 13] HONORÉ C., *The Slow Fix: Solve Problems, Work Smarter and Live Better in a Fast World*, Collins, 2013.

[HOR 93] HORN J., Finite Markov chain analysis of genetic algorithms with niching, IlliGAL Report no. 93002, University of Illinois, February 1993.

[HUS 91] HUSBADS P., MILL F., "Simulated co-evolution as the mechanism for emergent planning and scheduling", in *Proceedings of the Fourth International Conference on Genetic Algorithms (San Mateo, CA)*, Morgan Kaufman, pp. 264–270, 1991.

[IOA 04a] IOANNOU I., PERROT N., CURT C. *et al.*, "Development of a control system using the fuzzy set theory applied to a browning process – a fuzzy symbolic approach for the measurement of product browning: development of a diagnosis model – part I", *Journal of Food Engineering*, vol. 64, no. 4, pp. 497–506, 2004.

[IOA 04b] IOANNOU I., PERROT N., MAURIS G. *et al.*, "Development of a control system using the fuzzy set theory applied to a browning process – towards a control system of the browning process combining a diagnosis model and a decision model – part II", *Journal of Food Engineering*, vol. 64, no. 4, pp. 507–514, 2004.

[IOA 06] IOANNOU I., MAURIS G., TRYSTRAM G. *et al.*, "Back-propagation of imprecision in a cheese ripening fuzzy model based on human sensory evaluations", *Fuzzy Sets Syst.*, vol. 157, no. 9, pp. 1179–1187, 2006.

[JAM 13] JAMES W., STENGERS I., *Manifeste pour un ralentissement des sciences, suivi de le poulpe du doctorat*, Les Empcheurs de penser en rond, 2013.

[JAN 15] JANSEN Y., DRAGICEVIC P., ISENBERG P. *et al.*, "Opportunities and challenges for data physicalization", in *CHI 2015 – Proceedings of the SIGCHI Conference on Human Factors in Computing Systems*, Seoul, South Korea, ACM, April 2015.

[JIA 05] JIA H.-Y., LIU D.-Y., YU P., "Learning dynamic Bayesian network with immune evolutionary algorithm", in *International Conference on Machine Learning and Cybernetics*, vol. 5, pp. 2934–2938, 2005.

[JIM 05] JIMENEZ-MARQUEZ S., THIBAULT J., LACROIX C., "Prediction of moisture in cheese of commercial production using neural networks", *International Dairy Journal*, vol. 15, no. 11, pp. 1156–1174, 2005.

[JON 75] JONG K.A.D., Analysis of the behavior of a class of genetic adaptive systems, PhD thesis, University of Michigan, 1975.

[JON 13] JONES C.V., *Visualization and Optimization*, vol. 6, Springer Science & Business Media, 2013.

[KAM 97] KAMOHARA S., TAKAGI H., TAKEDA T., "Control rule acquisition for an arm wrestling robot", *IEEE Int. Conf. on System, Man and Cybernetics (SMC'97)*, Orlando, FL, vol. 5, 1997.

[KAU 92] KAUFFMAN S.A., JOHNSEN S., "Co-evolution to the edge of chaos: coupled fitness landscapes, poised states, and co-evolutionary avalanches", CHRISTOPHER G., LANGTON C., TAYLOR J.D.F., RASMUSSEN S. (eds), *Artificial Life II, Proceedings of the Workshop on Artificial Life Held February, 1990 in Santa Fe, New Mexico, Proceedings*, pp. 325–369, 1992.

[KNU 08] KNUDSEN J., OGENDAL L., SKIBSTED L., "Droplet surface properties and rheology of concentrated oil in water emulsions stabilized by heat-modified beta-lactoglobulin B", *Langmuir*, vol. 24, no. 6, pp. 2603–2610, 2008.

[KOZ 92] KOZA J.R., *Genetic Programming*, MIT Press, 1992.

[LAC 01] LACEY A., LUFF D., *Qualitative Data Analysis*, Trent Focus Sheffield, 2001.

[LAN 00a] LANDRIN-SCHWEITZER Y., LUTTON E., "Perturbation theory for evolutionary algorithms: towards an estimation of convergence speed", in SCHOENAUER M., DEB K., RUDOLF G. *et al.* (eds), *Parallel Problem Solving from Nature – PPSN VI 6th International Conference*, Paris, France, Springer Verlag, 16–20 September 2000.

[LAN 00b] LANGDON W.B., BANZHAF W., "Genetic programming bloat without semantics", in SCHOENAUER M., DEB K., RUDOLF G. *et al.*, (eds), *Parallel Problem Solving from Nature – PPSN VI 6th International Conference*, Paris, France, Springer Verlag, 16–20 September 2000.

[LAN 06] LANDRIN-SCHWEITZER Y., COLLET P., LUTTON E., "Introducing lateral thinking in search engines", *GPEM, Genetic Programming an Evolvable Hardware Journal*, vol. 1, no. 7, pp. 9–31, 2006.

[LAR 96a] LARRANAGA P. *et al.*, "Learning Bayesian network structures by searching for the best ordering with genetic algorithms", *Systems, Man and Cybernetics, Part A: Systems and Humans, IEEE Transactions on*, vol. 26, no. 4, pp. 487–493, 1996.

[LAR 96b] LARRANAGA P., POZA M., YURRAMENDI Y. *et al*, "Structure learning of Bayesian networks by genetic algorithms: a performance analysis of control parameters", *IEEE Transactions on Pattern Analysis and Machine Intelligence*, vol. 18, no. 9, pp. 912–926, 1996.

[LEB 98] LEBLANC B., LUTTON E., "Bitwise regularity and GA-hardness", in ICEC 98, Anchorage, Alaska, 5–9 May 1998.

[LEC 04] LECLERCQ-PERLAT M.-N., BUONO D., LAMBERT E. *et al.*, "Controlled production of Camembert-type cheeses. Part I: Microbiological and physicochemical evolutions", *J. Dairy Res.*, no. 71, pp. 346–354, 2004.

[LEC 16] LECLERCQ-PERLAT M.-N., PICQUE D., RIAHI H. *et al.*, "Microbiological and biochemical aspects of camembert-type cheeses depend on atmospheric composition in the ripening chamber", *Journal of Dairy Science*, vol. 89, no. 8, pp. 3260–3273, 2016.

[LEE 15] LEE C.-S., WANG M.-H.L.S.-T., "Adaptive personalized diet linguistic recommendation mechanism based on type-2 fuzzy sets and genetic fuzzy markup language", *IEEE Transactions on Fuzzy Systems*, vol. 23, no. 5, pp. 1777–1802, 2015.

[LEG 07] LEGRAND P., BOURGEOIS-REPUBLIQUE C., PEAN V. *et al.*, "Interactive evolution for cochlear implants fitting", *GPEM*, Special Issue on Medical Applications, vol. 8, no. 4, pp. 319–354, 2007.

[LEH 11] LEHMAN J., STANLEY K.O., "Abandoning objectives: evolution through the search for novelty alone", *Evol. Comput.*, vol. 19, no. 2, pp. 189–223, 2011.

[LEN 84] LENOIR J., "The surface flora and its role in the ripening of cheese", *Int Dairy Fed Bull*, no. 171, pp. 3–20, 1984.

[LIU 14] LIU DAN, SUN D.-W. Z. X.-A., "Recent advances in wavelength selection techniques for hyperspectral image processing in the food industry", *Food and Bioprocess Technology*, vol. 7, no. 2, pp. 307–323, 2014.

[LOB 05] LOBO F.G., LIMA C.F., "A review of adaptive population sizing schemes in genetic algorithms", in *Proceedings of the 7th Annual Workshop on Genetic and Evolutionary Computation*, GECCO '05, New York, ACM, pp. 228–234, 2005.

[LOU 02] LOUCHET J., GUYON M., LESOT M.-J. *et al.*, "Dynamic flies: a new pattern recognition tool applied to stereo sequence processing", *Pattern Recogn. Lett.*, vol. 23, nos. 1–3, pp. 335–345, January 2002.

[LUT 96] LUTTON E., MARTINEZ P., "A genetic algorithm with sharing for the detection of 2D geometric primitives in images", in ALLIOT J-M., LUTTON E., RONALD E. *et al.* (eds), *Artificial Evolution: European Conference, AE 95 Brest, France, September 4–6, 1995*, Springer, Berlin, Heidelberg, pp. 287–303, 1996.

[LUT 06a] LUTTON E., LÉVY VÉHEL J., "Pointwise regularity of fitness landscapes and the performance of a simple ES", in *CEC'06*, Vancouver, Canada, 16–21 July 2006.

[LUT 06b] LUTTON E., LANDRIN-SCHWEITZER Y., LÉVY VÉHEL J., Experiments on controlled regularity fitness landscapes, Report no. RR-5823, INRIA Rocquencourt, February 2006.

[LUT 11a] LUTTON E., FEKETE J.-D., "Visual Analytics of EA Data", in *Genetic and Evolutionary Computation Conference, GECCO 2011*, Dublin, Ireland, 12–16 July 2011.

[LUT 11b] LUTTON E., FOUCQUIER J., PERROT N. *et al.*, "Visual analysis of population scatterplots", in *10th Biannual International Conference on Artificial Evolution (EA-2011)*, Angers, France, 2011.

[LUT 14a] LUTTON E., GILBERT H., CANCINO W., *et al.*, "GridVis: visualisation of island-based parallel genetic algorithms", in *Evopar2014, EvoApplications track of EvoStar*, Springer, Granada, Spain, 23–25 April 2014.

[LUT 14b] LUTTON E., TONDA A., GAUCEL S., *et al.*, "Food model exploration through evolutionary optimization coupled with visualization: application to the prediction of a milk gel structure", *Innovative Food Science & Emerging Technologies*, vol. 25, pp. 67–77, 2014.

[MAR 64] MARCUSE H., *Industrialization and Capitalism*, http://newleftreview.org/static/assets/archive/pdf-bak/NLR02901.pdf, 1964.

[MAR 78] MARKWELL A., HAAS S., BIEBER L. *et al.*, "Modification of Lowry procedure to simplify protein determination in membrane and lipoprotein samples", *Analytical Biochemistry*, vol. 87, no. 1, pp. 206–210, 1978.

[MAR 02] MARTIN M., *La nature est un livre écrit en langage mathématique*, Galilée, Pleins Feux, 2002.

[MAU 84] MAULDIN M.L., "Maintening diversity in genetic search.", *Proceedings of the National Conference on Artificial Intelligence*, 1984.

[MCC 04] MCCLEMENTS D., "Protein-stabilized emulsions", *Current opinion in Colloid & Interface Science*, vol. 9, no. 5, pp. 305–313, 2004.

[MIC 92] MICHALEWICZ Z., *Genetic Algorithms + Data Structures = Evolution Programs*, Springer Verlag, New York, 1992.

[MOH 11a] MOHEBBI MOHEBBAT, FATHI M.S.F., "Genetic algorithm-artificial neural network modeling of moisture and oil content of pretreated fried mushroom", *Food and Bioprocess Technology*, vol. 4, no. 4, pp. 603–609, 2011.

[MOH 11b] MOHEBBI M., AKBARZADEH-T.M.-R.S.-F.E.A., "Modeling and optimization of mass transfer during osmosis dehydration of carrot slices by neural networks and genetic algorithms", *International Journal of Food Engineering*, vol. 7, no. 2, 2011.

[MON 99] MONMARCHE N., NOCENT G., VENTURINI G. *et al.*, "Generating HTML style sheets with an interactive genetic algorithm based on gene frequencies", *Artificial Evolution, European Conference, AE 99, Dunkerque, France, November 1999, Selected papers*, Springer Verlag, 1999.

[MOR 12] MORAND M., DEKKARI A., GUYOMARC'H F. *et al.*, "Increasing the hydrophobicity of the heat-induced whey protein complexes improves the acid gelation of skim milk", *International Dairy Journal*, vol. 25, no. 2, pp. 103–111, 2012.

[MUR 01] MURPHY K.P., "The Bayes net toolbox for MATLAB", *Computing Science and Statistics*, vol. 33, pp. 1024–1034, 2001.

[MUR 02] MURRAY B., "Interfacial rheology of food emulsifiers and proteins", *Current Opinion in Colloid & Interface Science*, vol. 7, nos. 5–6, pp. 426–431, 2002.

[MYE 99] MYERS J.W., LASKEY K.B., DEJONG K.A., "Learning Bayesian networks from incomplete data using evolutionary algorithms", *Proceedings of the 1st Annual Conference on Genetic and Evolutionary Computation*, GECCO'99, San Francisco, CA, Morgan Kaufmann, vol. 1, pp. 458–465, 1999.

[NAK 16] NAKANDALA DILUPA, LAU H.Z.-J., "Cost-optimization modeling for fresh food quality and transportation", *Industrial Management & Data Systems*, vol. 116, no. 3, pp. 564–583, 2016.

[NER 12] NERI F., COTTA C., "Memetic algorithms and memetic computing optimization: a literature review", *Swarm and Evolutionary Computation*, vol. 2, pp. 1–14, 2012.

[NGU 09] NGUYEN Q.H., ONG Y.-S., LIM M.H., "A probabilistic memetic framework", *Evolutionary Computation, IEEE Transactions on*, vol. 13, no. 3, pp. 604–623, 2009.

[NI 98] NI H., GUNASEKARAN S., "Food quality prediction with neural networks", *Food Technology*, vol. 52, pp. 60–65, 1998.

[NIX 92] NIX A., VOSE M., "Modeling genetic algorithms with Markov chains", *Annals of Mathematics and Artificial Intelligence*, vol. 5, no. 1, pp. 79–88, 1992.

[NOR 91] NORMAN M., MOSCATO P., "A competitive and cooperative approach to complex combinatorial search", in *Proceedings of the 20th Informatics and Operations Research Meeting*, pp. 3–15, 1991.

[OCH 07] OCHOA G., LUTTON E., BURKE E.K., "Cooperative Royal Road Functions", *Evolution Artificielle*, Tours, France, 29–31 October 2007.

[OCH 08] OCHOA G., LUTTON E., BURKE E., *The Cooperative Royal Road: Avoiding Hitchhiking*, Springer, Berlin, Heidelberg, pp. 184–195, 2008.

[ONE 03] O'NEILL M., RYAN C., *Grammatical Evolution: Evolutionary Automatic Programming in an Arbitrary Language*, Kluwer Academic Publishers, Norwell, 2003.

[PAN 06] PANAIT L., LUKE S., HARRISON J.F., "Archive-based cooperative coevolutionary algorithms", in *Proceedings of the 8th Annual Conference on Genetic and Evolutionary Computation*, GECCO '06, New York, USA, ACM, pp. 345–352, 2006.

[PAT 86] PATTON S., HUSTON G., "A method for isolation of milk-fat globules", *Lipids*, vol. 21, no. 2, pp. 170–174, 1986.

[PAU 02] PAUL R., WIEGAND R.P., JONG K.A.D., *et al.*, "Analyzing cooperative coevolution with evolutionary game theory", in *Proceedings of the 2002 Congress on Evolutionary Computation*, 2002.

[PEA 91] PEARL J., VERMA T., "A Theory of inferred causation", *2nd International Conference on the Principles of Knowledge Representation and Reasoning*, 1991.

[PER 11] PERROT N., TRELEA I., BAUDRIT C. *et al.*, "Modeling and analysis of complex food systems: state of the art and new trends", *Trends in Food Science & Technology*, vol. 22, no. 6, pp. 304–314, 2011.

[PER 16] PERROT N., VRIES H.D., LUTTON E. *et al.*, "Some remarks on computational approaches towards sustainable complex agri-food systems", *Trends in Food Science and Technology*, vol. 48, pp. 88–101, 2016.

[PIN 08] PINAUD B., BAUDRIT C., SICARD M. *et al.*, "Validation et enrichissement interactifs d'un apprentissage automatique des paramètres d'un réseau bayésien dynamique appliqué aux procédés alimentaires", *Journées Francophone sur les Réseaux Bayésiens*, Lyon, France, 2008.

[POP 06] POPOVICI E., DE JONG K., "The effects of interaction frequency on the optimization performance of cooperative coevolution", in *Proceedings of the 8th Annual Conference on Genetic and Evolutionary Computation*, GECCO '06, New York, USA, ACM, pp. 353–360, 2006.

[POT 00] POTTER M.A., JONG K.A.D., "Cooperative coevolution: an architecture for evolving coadapted subcomponents", *Evolutionary Computation*, vol. 8, pp. 1–29, 2000.

[POT 10] POTTER A., MCCLURE M., SELLERS K., "Mass collaboration problem solving: A new approach to wicked problems", in *Collaborative Technologies and Systems (CTS), 2010 International Symposium*, pp. 398–407, 2010.

[PRU 01] "Modeling GA dynamics", *Theoretical Aspects of Evolutionary Computing: Proceedings of the Second EvoNet Summer School, Antwerp, 1999*, Springer, pp. 59–86, 2001.

[RAB 11] RABE M., VERDES D., SEEGER S., "Understanding protein adsorption phenomena at solid surfaces", *Advances in Colloid and Interface Science*, vol. 162, nos. 1–2, pp. 87–106, 2011.

[RAD 15] RADY AHMED, GUYER D., "Utilization of visible/near-infrared spectroscopic and wavelength selection methods in sugar prediction and potatoes classification", *Journal of Food Measurement and Characterization*, vol. 9, no. 1, pp. 20–34, 2015.

[REC 73] RECHENBERG I., *Evolutionsstrategie: Optimierung Technicher System nach Prinzipien der Biologischen Evolution*, Fromman Holzboog, Stuttgart, 1973.

[REC 89] RECHENBERG I., "Evolution strategy: nature's way of optimization", *Optimization: Methods and Applications. Possibilities and Limitations*, Springer, Berlin, vol. 17, pp. 106–126, 1989.

[REE 00] REEVES C.R., "Experiments with tuneable fitness landscapes", in SCHOENAUER M., DEB K., RUDOLF G. *et al.* (eds), *Parallel Problem Solving from Nature – PPSN VI 6th International Conference*, Paris, France, Springer Verlag, 16–20 September 2000.

[REG 12] REGNIER-COUDERT O., MCCALL J., "An Island model genetic algorithm for Bayesian network structure learning", *IEEE CEC*, pp. 1–8, 2012.

[RIA 07] RIAHI M., TRELEA I., LECLERCQ-PERLAT M.-N. *et al.*, "Model for changes in weight and dry matter during the ripening of a smear soft cheese under controlled temperature and relative humidity", *International Dairy Journal*, vol. 17, no. 8, pp. 946–953, 2007.

[ROB 77] ROBINSON R.W., "*Counting unlabeled acyclic digraphs*", in LITTLE C.H.E. (ed.), *Combinational Methamatics V*, Springer, Berlin, Heidelberg, 1977.

[ROS 32] ROSTAND J., *L'évolution des espèces. Histoire des idées transformistes*, Hachette, 1932.

[ROS 67] ROSENBERG R.S., Simulation of genetic populations with biochemical properties, PhD thesis, University of Michigan, 1967.

[ROS 07] ROSS B.J., ZUVIRIA E., "Evolving dynamic Bayesian networks with multi-objective genetic algorithms", *Applied Intelligence*, vol. 26, no. 1, pp. 13–23, 2007.

[SAL 02] SALTELLI A., "Making best use of model evaluations to compute sensitivity indices", *Computer Physics Communications*, vol. 145, no. 2, pp. 280–297, 2002.

[SCH 75] SCHWEFEL H.P., Evolutionsstrategie und numerische Optimierung, PhD thesis, Technische Universitat, Berlin, May 1975.

[SCH 95] SCHWEFEL H.-P., *Numerical Optimization of Computer Models*, 2nd ed., John Wiley & Sons, New-York, 1995.

[SCH 96] SCHLIERKAMP-VOOSEN D., MUHLENBEIN H., "Adaptation of population sizes by competing subpopulations", in *Evolutionary Computation, Proceedings of IEEE International Conference on*, pp. 330–335, 1996.

[SHA 96] SHAPIRO J., RATTRAY M., PRGEL-BENNETT A., "The statistical mechanics theory of genetic algorithm dynamics", *First International Conference on Evolutionary Computation and its Applications*, Moscow, Plenary Lecture, 1996.

[SIL 05] SILVA S., ALMEIDA J., "Gplab-a genetic programming toolbox for matlab", *In Proc. of the Nordic MATLAB Conference (NMC-2003)*, pp. 273–278, http://gplab.sourceforge.net/, 2005.

[SIM 91a] SIMS K., "Interactive evolution of dynamical systems", in *First European Conference on Artificial Life*, Paris, pp. 171–178, December 1991.

[SIM 91b] SIMS K., "Artificial evolution for computer graphics", *Computer Graphics*, vol. 25, no. 4, pp. 319–328, 1991.

[SIM 08] SIMONS C., PARMEE I., "User-centered, evolutionary search in conceptual software design", in *Evolutionary Computation, 2008. CEC 2008. IEEE Congress on*, pp. 869–876, June 2008.

[SOU 96] SOULE T., FOSTER J.A., DICKINSON J., "Code growth in genetic programming", in KOZA J.R., GOLDBERG D.E., FOGEL D.B. *et al.*, (eds), *Genetic Programming 1996: Proceedings of the First Annual Conference*, Stanford University, CA, USA, pp. 215–223, 1996.

[SPI 01] SPIRTES P., GLYMOUR C., SCHEINES R., *Causation, Prediction, and Search, 2nd Edition*, vol. 1, MIT Press, 2001.

[SUG 81] SUGIYAMA K., TAGAWA S., TODA M., "Methods for visual understanding of hierarchical system structures", *IEEE Transactions on Systems, Man, and Cybernetics*, vol. SMC-11, no. 2, pp. 109–125, 1981.

[SUR 14] SUREL C., FOUCQUIER J., PERROT N. *et al.*, "Composition and structure of interface impacts texture of O/W emulsions", *Food Hydrocolloids*, vol. 34, pp. 3–9, 2014.

[TAK 98] TAKAGI H., "Interactive evolutionary computation: system optimisation based on human subjective evaluation", in *IEEE Int. Conf. on Intelligent Engineering Systems (INES'98)*, Vienna, Austria, 17–19 September 1998.

[TAK 99] TAKAGI H., OHSAKI M., "IEC-based hearing aids fitting", in *IEEE Int. Conf. on System, Man and Cybernetics (SMC'99)*, Tokyo, Japan, vol. 3, 12–15 October 1999.

[TAK 01] TAKAGI H., "Interactive evolutionary computation as humanized computational intelligence technology", in *Computational Intelligence. Theory and Applications*, Springer, p. 1, 2001.

[TAK 08] TAKAGI H., "New topics from recent interactive evolutionary computation researches", in *Knowledge-Based Int. Information and Eng. Systems*, p. 14, 2008.

[TAR 05] TARANTILIS C., KIRANOUDIS C., "Operational research and food logistics", *Journal of Food Engineering*, vol. 70, no. 3, pp. 253–255, 2005.

[TOD 92] TODD S., LATHAM W., *Evolutionary Art and Computers*, Academic Press, 1992.

[TON 12] TONDA A.P., LUTTON E., REUILLON R. *et al.*, "Bayesian network structure learning from limited datasets through graph evolution", in *EuroGP*, Springer Verlag, Malaga, Spain, 11–13 April 2012.

[TON 13a] TONDA A., LUTTON E., WUILLHEMIN P. *et al.*, "A memetic approach to Bayesian network structure learning", in ESPARCIA-ALCAZAR A.E.A., (ed.), *EvoApplications 2013*, European Conference on the Applications of Evolutionary Computation of *LNCS*, Springer-Verlag, 2013.

[TON 13b] TONDA A., SPRITZER A., LUTTON E., "Balancing user interaction and control in Bayesian network structure learning", in *11th Biannual International Conference on Artificial Evolution (EA-2013)*, Bordeaux, France, 21–23 October 2013.

[TRI 14] TRINCA L.C., CAPRARU A.-M.A.-D.E.A., "Monitoring methods and predictive models for water status in Jonathan apples", *Food Chemistry*, vol. 144, pp. 80–86, 2014.

[TUC 99] TUCKER A., LIU X., "Extending evolutionary programming methods to the learning of dynamic Bayesian networks", *GECCO '99*, 1999.

[VÉH 93] VÉHEL J.L., LUTTON E., "Optimization of fractal functions using genetic algorithms", *Fractal 93*, London, 1993.

[VAN 14] VAN MIL H., FOEGEDING E., WINDHAB E., *et al.*, "A complex system approach to address world challenges in food and agriculture", *Trends in Food Science and Technology*, vol. 40, no. 1, pp. 20–32, 2014.

[VID 13] VIDAILLET B., *Evaluez-moi! Evaluation au travail: les ressorts d'une fascination*, Le Seuil, 2013.

[VOS 90] VOSE M., "Formalizing genetic algorithms", in *Genetic Algorithms, Neural Networks and Simulated Annealing Applied to Problems in Signal and Image Processing*, IEEE, University of Glasgow, 8–9 May 1990.

[VOU 11] VOULGARI I., KOMIS V., "On studying collaborative learning interactions in massively multiplayer online games", in *Games and Virtual Worlds for Serious Applications (VS-GAMES), 2011 Third International Conference on*, pp. 182–183, May 2011.

[VRI 10] VRIES H.D., DARBISHIRE A.D., FARMER J.B., *The Mutation Theory, Experiments and Observations on the Origin of Species in the Vegetable Kingdom*, vol. 2, Open Court Publishing Company, Chicago, 1910.

[WAN 04] WANG S.-C., LI S.-P., *Learning Bayesian Networks by Lamarckian Genetic Algorithm and its Application to Yeast Cell-cycle Gene Network Reconstruction from Time-series Microarray Data*, Springer, Berlin, Heidelberg, pp. 49–62, 2004.

[WIE 06] WIEGAND R.P., POTTER M.A., "Robustness in cooperative coevolution", in *Proceedings of the 8th annual conference on Genetic and Evolutionary Computation*, Seattle, Washington, USA, 2006.

[WIL 06] WILLIAMS L., AMANT R.S., "A visualization technique for Bayesian modeling", in *Proceedings of IUI'06*, 2006.

[WOI 14] WOINAROSCHY A., "IMultiobjective optimal design for biodiesel sustainable production", *Fuel*, vol. 135, pp. 393–405, 2014.

[WON 99] WONG M.L., LAM W., LEUNG K.S., "Using evolutionary programming and minimum description length principle for data mining of Bayesian networks", *Pattern Analysis and Machine Intelligence, IEEE Trans. on*, vol. 21, no. 2, pp. 174–178, 1999.

[WON 04] WONG M.L., LEUNG K.S., "An efficient data mining method for learning Bayesian networks using an evolutionary algorithm-based hybrid approach", *IEEE Transactions on Evolutionary Computation*, vol. 8, no. 4, pp. 378–404, 2004.

[ZIT 00] ZITZLER E., DEB K., THIELE L., "Comparison of multiobjective evolutionary algorithms: empirical results", *Evolutionary Computation*, vol. 8, no. 2, pp. 173–195, 2000.

Index

Other titles from

in

Computer Engineering

2016

BLUM Christian, FESTA Paola
Metaheuristics for String Problems in Bio-informatics
(Metaheuristics Set – Volume 6)

DEROUSSI Laurent
Metaheuristics for Logistics
(Metaheuristics Set Volume 4)

DHAENENS Clarisse and JOURDAN Laetitia
Metaheuristics for Big Data (Metaheuristics set – Volume 5)

LABADIE Nacima, PRINS Christian, PRODHON Caroline
Metaheuristics for Vehicle Routing Problems
(Metaheuristics Set – Volume 3)

LEROY Laure
Eyestrain Reduction in Stereoscopy

MAGOULÈS Frédéric, ZHAO Hai-Xiang
Data Mining and Machine Learning in Building Energy Analysis

OUSSALAH Mourad Chabane
Software Architecture 1
Software Architecture 2

PASCHOS Vangelis Th
Combinatorial Optimization – 3-volume series, 2nd Edition
Concepts of Combinatorial Optimization – Volume 1, 2nd Edition
Problems and New Approaches – Volume 2, 2nd Edition
Applications of Combinatorial Optimization – Volume 3, 2nd Edition

QUESNEL Flavien
Scheduling of Large-scale Virtualized Infrastructures: Toward Cooperative Management

RIGO Michel
Formal Languages, Automata and Numeration Systems 1: Introduction to Combinatorics on Words
Formal Languages, Automata and Numeration Systems 2: Applications to Recognizability and Decidability

SAINT-DIZIER Patrick
Musical Rhetoric: Foundations and Annotation Schemes

TOUATI Sid, DE DINECHIN Benoit
Advanced Backend Optimization

2013

ANDRÉ Etienne, SOULAT Romain
The Inverse Method: Parametric Verification of Real-time Embedded Systems

BOULANGER Jean-Louis
Safety Management for Software-based Equipment

DELAHAYE Daniel, PUECHMOREL Stéphane
Modeling and Optimization of Air Traffic

FRANCOPOULO Gil
LMF — Lexical Markup Framework

GHÉDIRA Khaled
Constraint Satisfaction Problems

ROCHANGE Christine, UHRIG Sascha, SAINRAT Pascal
Time-Predictable Architectures

WAHBI Mohamed
Algorithms and Ordering Heuristics for Distributed Constraint Satisfaction Problems

ZELM Martin *et al.*
Enterprise Interoperability

2012

ARBOLEDA Hugo, ROYER Jean-Claude
Model-Driven and Software Product Line Engineering

BLANCHET Gérard, DUPOUY Bertrand
Computer Architecture

BOULANGER Jean-Louis
Industrial Use of Formal Methods: Formal Verification

BOULANGER Jean-Louis
Formal Method: Industrial Use from Model to the Code

CALVARY Gaëlle, DELOT Thierry, SÈDES Florence, TIGLI Jean-Yves
Computer Science and Ambient Intelligence

MAHOUT Vincent
Assembly Language Programming: ARM Cortex-M3 2.0: Organization, Innovation and Territory

MARLET Renaud
Program Specialization

SOTO Maria, SEVAUX Marc, ROSSI André, LAURENT Johann
Memory Allocation Problems in Embedded Systems: Optimization Methods

2011

BICHOT Charles-Edmond, SIARRY Patrick
Graph Partitioning

BOULANGER Jean-Louis
Static Analysis of Software: The Abstract Interpretation

CAFERRA Ricardo
Logic for Computer Science and Artificial Intelligence

HOMES Bernard
Fundamentals of Software Testing

KORDON Fabrice, HADDAD Serge, PAUTET Laurent, PETRUCCI Laure
Distributed Systems: Design and Algorithms

KORDON Fabrice, HADDAD Serge, PAUTET Laurent, PETRUCCI Laure
Models and Analysis in Distributed Systems

LORCA Xavier
Tree-based Graph Partitioning Constraint

TRUCHET Charlotte, ASSAYAG Gerard
Constraint Programming in Music

VICAT-BLANC PRIMET Pascale *et al.*
Computing Networks: From Cluster to Cloud Computing

2010

AUDIBERT Pierre
Mathematics for Informatics and Computer Science

BABAU Jean-Philippe *et al.*
Model Driven Engineering for Distributed Real-Time Embedded Systems 2009

BOULANGER Jean-Louis
Safety of Computer Architectures

MONMARCHE Nicolas *et al.*
Artificial Ants

PANETTO Hervé, BOUDJLIDA Nacer
Interoperability for Enterprise Software and Applications 2010

PASCHOS Vangelis Th
Combinatorial Optimization – 3-volume series
Concepts of Combinatorial Optimization – Volume 1
Problems and New Approaches – Volume 2
Applications of Combinatorial Optimization – Volume 3

SIGAUD Olivier *et al.*
Markov Decision Processes in Artificial Intelligence

SOLNON Christine
Ant Colony Optimization and Constraint Programming

AUBRUN Christophe, SIMON Daniel, SONG Ye-Qiong *et al.*
Co-design Approaches for Dependable Networked Control Systems

2009

FOURNIER Jean-Claude
Graph Theory and Applications

GUEDON Jeanpierre
The Mojette Transform / Theory and Applications

JARD Claude, ROUX Olivier
Communicating Embedded Systems / Software and Design

LECOUTRE Christophe
Constraint Networks / Targeting Simplicity for Techniques and Algorithms

2008

BANÂTRE Michel, MARRÓN Pedro José, OLLERO Hannibal, WOLITZ Adam
Cooperating Embedded Systems and Wireless Sensor Networks

MERZ Stephan, NAVET Nicolas
Modeling and Verification of Real-time Systems

PASCHOS Vangelis Th
Combinatorial Optimization and Theoretical Computer Science: Interfaces and Perspectives

WALDNER Jean-Baptiste
Nanocomputers and Swarm Intelligence

2007

BENHAMOU Frédéric, JUSSIEN Narendra, O'SULLIVAN Barry
Trends in Constraint Programming

JUSSIEN Narendra
A to Z of Sudoku

2006

BABAU Jean-Philippe *et al.*
From MDD Concepts to Experiments and Illustrations – DRES 2006

HABRIAS Henri, FRAPPIER Marc
Software Specification Methods

MURAT Cecile, PASCHOS Vangelis Th
Probabilistic Combinatorial Optimization on Graphs

PANETTO Hervé, BOUDJLIDA Nacer
Interoperability for Enterprise Software and Applications 2006 / IFAC-IFIP I-ESA'2006

2005

GÉRARD Sébastien *et al.*
Model Driven Engineering for Distributed Real Time Embedded Systems

PANETTO Hervé
Interoperability of Enterprise Software and Applications 2005

CPSIA information can be obtained
at www.ICGtesting.com
Printed in the USA
BVOW06*0820301116

469235BV00005B/8/P